# WOUNDED

## A LEGACY OF OPERATION IRAQI FREEDOM

## CAPTAIN ED 'RIV' HRIVNAK
## AIR FORCE FLIGHT NURSE

ISBN: 1482394979
ISBN 13: 9781482394979
Library of Congress Control Number: 2013903415
CreateSpace Independent Publishing Platform
North Charleston, SC

# Support Heartbeat- Serving Wounded Warriors

We provide emergency assistance, therapeutic services, and morale-building programs for wounded service members and their families in Washington State. Our focus is on the wounded and injured. *Heartbeat* is a private, 501(c)(3) nonprofit organization — donations are tax deductible as allowed by law.

We offer programs to wounded and injured service members from all branches of the military. Please visit http://www.heartbeatforwarriors.org/ and find out how you can help our veterans.

# About the Cover:

"Baghdad at Sunrise" is an original oil painting by Lt. Colonel Rob Chatfield. This artist rendition is of a C-141C medevac flight waiting for wounded on June 28, 2003. The jet is tail number 7955, an active duty aircraft that was crewed by personnel from McGuire Air Force Base, New Jersey. The aeromedical evacuation crew and critical care air transport team are a composite of reservists. The aircrew held over past the cover of darkness to load thirty-eight casualties. The wounded resulted from multiple ambushes after fires were set to lure the soldiers.

Colonel Chatfield is a retired air force aviator who piloted combat and aeromedical missions spanning the globe during his thirty-three years of service. Chatfield saw his first wounded soldier while flying into Saigon. His career was littered with conflicts, including operations in Vietnam, Desert Storm, Somalia, Haiti, Iraqi Freedom, and Afghanistan. After flying over ten thousand hours, he settled on South Pender Island Canada with his wife, Nancy. Rob attended the Victoria College of Art, completing a diploma in Fine Arts, and studied at the Master's level. He operates a studio with a view of the San Juan Islands. Rob also orchestrates an outreach program that teaches disabled veterans to scuba dive on the shores of his home.

The artist and author are colleagues and close friends that served in the same Air Wing for fourteen years.

# Introduction

This book is dedicated to the men and women who have fought since the world changed on September 11, 2001. Many either gave their lives or were wounded. Some still struggle with physical and mental scars. All who served, and their families, were changed in some way.

During Operation Iraqi Freedom, I kept a running journal of my experiences during the war. It started as simple e-mails to friends and family. One friend asked if she could publish part of the journal. It ended up in the *Tacoma News Tribune*. The *Tribune* article encouraged me to refine the journal. E-mails transformed into short stories.

Much of the journal was written post mission while sleep deprived, so there are bound to be inaccuracies.

The more I wrote the more responses I received. Stories were forwarded to others. Letters were read in classrooms and Boy Scout meetings, where they were discussed and debated. Soon I had thank-you letters of support from people I'd never met. More publications picked up the stories, and within months parts of the journal were printed in over a dozen different newspapers and magazines. There was a smattering of overseas publications in Germany and England.

Some of my best work was later published in the anthology *Operation Homecoming*, a veterans' writing initiative by the National Endowment of the Arts. I was very fortunate to be selected from thousands of submissions. Eleven of us had our stories produced into short movies for a full-length, theatrical film by the Peter Jennings Documentary Group.

The main purpose of this book is to fill the gaps between the stories, to give the reader a behind-the-scenes look at what it was like to evacuate the wounded at the start of Operation Iraqi Freedom. I want you to understand the price of war.

The foundation of this narrative is the idea that any casualty statistic mentioned in the news represents a real person. A wounded soldier is a human being, vulnerable and weakened. Those who care for them, at times struggling to maintain *life*, are also scarred. These men and women are an incredible source of strength, courage, and devotion. This is my testament to them.

# Contents

# HOW DID I GET HERE?

I'm looking at a forearm. The skin has no tan, which tells me the young soldier hasn't been in-country long. I'm holding his arm, searching for a place to insert a needle. The ground crews, rushed to load the plane under the cover of darkness, tore out this ranger's IV as they unloaded the Humvee ambulance.

He is dehydrated and the veins are collapsed. I can't see or feel them. I tighten the tourniquet around his arm. He doesn't flinch. Beads of sweat roll off his face from a combination of the heat and pain.

I want to implant a sixteen gauge needle, but I'm not confidant I can find the vein. I settle for the smaller eighteen gauge to ensure success. The boy is on the bottom tier, so I'm on my knees. The dirty greasy cargo floor is my work area for sterile medical supplies. The floor is slick from the mix of desert sand and freely sweating bodies. I cannot feel the needle in hands covered by latex gloves. Salty, wet sand finds its way into every crevice of cracked skin.

The GI is in pain, but he neither screams nor complains. A soft, muffled moan escapes from his lips. I push the needle where I think the vein should be and immediately get a flash of blood. My medic, Steve, oversees and, without asking, has a bag of fluid ready to stick in the catheter.

I stretch for a brown paper bag tossed on its side with vials of narcotics and antibiotics spilling out of the top. Drawing up a syringe with ten milligrams of morphine, I push six into the soldier's vein. He relaxes, and we both receive satisfaction. I tape the remaining four milligrams next to his head, knowing that he will get that, plus more.

I stand up slowly. My knees creak from kneeling, and my back is sore from months of lifting body-laden stretchers. I look down the line of stacked wounded on litters. I have spent too much time with this patient. The eleven other casualties I've been assigned are waiting for care. I'm thinking, "How did I get here?"

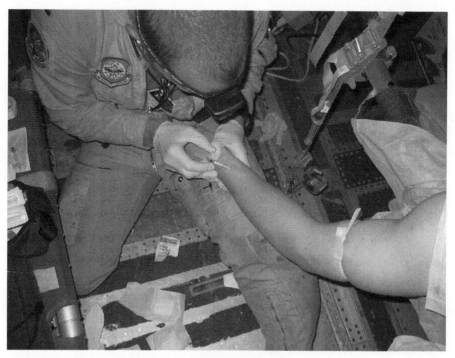

Starting an IV line on the floor of the plane

# Prelude to War

## 1998 - 2001

I was an instructor in the Air Force Reserve. Flight nurses typically work about a hundred days a year as traditional reservists. Besides working one weekend a month and a two-week summer camp, we have to maintain proficiency flying. This involves travelling anywhere in the world and transporting patients to and from military hospitals. In peacetime, the aeromedical evacuation flights are fairly mundane and involve caring for stable patients. This could be a pregnant woman or a retiree with a heart condition. It is a controlled environment. The missions last anywhere from one to ten days. Often, we have no patients and train on mannequins or each other.

In 1998, the air force added a new cargo jet to the fleet. In 1999, I was assigned to Charleston, South Carolina, for training on the aircraft. Our wing had begun to convert to the C-17 cargo plane, a high-tech jet that could land in austere places, even directly in the combat zone. The instructors brainstormed about war and what it would be like to fly in a combat environment. We wrote talking papers on the type of training needed for the next war. We presented these ideas to our squadron commander. Our ideas were rejected.

# August 2001

With resistance, Major Rob Richardson convinced the McChord Reserve Wing to participate in a navy exercise called SEAHAWK 2001. The military training involved dozens of agencies and hundreds of military and civilian personnel. The drill was designed to simulate a large-scale terrorist attack against the United States. For two weeks, aircrews and medical teams moved hundreds of pretend casualties in a realistic, terrorist-based war scenario. Helicopters and various ground and air transports brought patients to one central location at McChord Air Force Base (AFB) in Tacoma, Washington. We even used landing craft and boats to move victims on the Puget Sound. The wounded were triaged and loaded en masse on C-141 transports to evac to regional hospitals.

After the exercise, the instructors talked about the lessons learned and what to do for the next year. Our squadron commander stated that we didn't need this kind of exercise again. The colonel didn't think it was realistic. A relic of the Vietnam War, she did not foresee how the next war would be fought. Before we could resolve how to train reservists, terrorists forced us to learn on the job.

# The Global War on Terrorism Begins

## September 11, 2001

The ringing phone woke Jennifer and me. My mom was crying on the other end of the line. She said to turn on the news.

"It had blown up."

"What had blown up?"

I didn't get what she was saying. Mom blurted, "Turn on the news!"

I ran downstairs with the phone and turned on CNN. We watched one of the Twin Towers burning for a few minutes. I said a few words to my mom, trying to comprehend what was happening. While we watched, a jetliner hit the second tower. Then I knew . . . we were at war. "Mom, we have to go, we have work to do."

I looked at Jennifer and told her we needed to start packing. She was also a reserve flight nurse. Reservists maintain a mobility bag to deploy within twenty-four hours' notice. Our bags weren't ready. She didn't understand. I searched for my flight boots and extra flight suits while Jennifer stood there, watching me pack. Tears welled in her eyes.

"What does this mean?"

I stood up from the closet and told her, "Jennifer, our country has been attacked. I don't know by who or why. We are at war and needed to get ready to deploy."

She came over to me, and we held each other. She cried. I wanted to cry, but choked to keep it in. We held each other. Our lives would never be the same. That horrific moment in time when the Twin Towers fell forever changed us. It was one of the defining moments of our marriage. The four years we had known each other had been care-free up to this point. We continued packing.

Four hours later, the phone rang. It was the reserve squadron. The admin clerk wanted to know if we were willing to deploy for two weeks to evac the expected casualties from New York and the Pentagon. I said we were packed and set to go. As a married couple, Jennifer and I could not fly on the same airplane, so she was scheduled to fly out at midnight and I would leave at noon, September 12. We were instructed to stay in phone contact and not to drive onto McChord AFB. The base was locked down and only mission-essential personnel could enter.

We were now on active duty and in BRAVO alert, meaning that we needed to be airborne within three hours of being called.

As the day dragged on, other friends from the Reserves called to see what was happening. No one knew. There was a communication blackout and lots of rumors. Our house was close to base, so reservists started to drift over, and we watched the news together. Media speculated there could be as many as ten thousand casualties. I tried to comprehend the numbers. How many patients would we have on each plane? What would be their injuries? How long would it take us to evacuate ten thousand people?

We elected to boat on the lake. Watching the never-ending TV coverage was damaging our psyches. The squadron could call us on the cell phone.

The weather was warm and still. Even the birds did not respond, sensing the tragedy. We were the only ones on Spanaway Lake; everyone else was watching TV. Our days on the lake were numbered, so we spent the time wakeboarding. It kept our minds off what would come.

That evening, the squadron called and said our mission was delayed. We remained in BRAVO and waited.

No word came on September 12, just rumors. We waited. Slowly, over the next several days, it dawned on us that there were no large volumes of wounded. The injured were treated at local hospitals. There would be no mass casualty evacuation. The urban rescue teams were not finding hundreds of trapped survivors, only body parts.

On September 26, we were released from active duty. Our mobility bags remained packed and sat in the closet. It was just a matter of time before we went overseas. Jennifer and I prepared for a long time apart.

## February 14, 2003: *Colin Powell addresses the United Nations Security Council.- CNN*

After September 11, our squadron shipped a few dozen volunteers to different countries to support the War on Terrorism. The assignments were ninety days, and the missions were small patient loads. As time passed, it was clear that we were heading for Iraq as large numbers of reservists were recalled to duty.

My primary job during war was working the crew management cell (CMC). I would sit in an office in some forward location and assign needed medevac crews to a casualty mission. It was a thankless job that I'd recently been promoted into. Aircrews are rarely satisfied with staff decisions.

Jan, our operations officer, called me and asked what my preference was if our squadron mobilized.

"Where are you going with this?"

She said, "My friends at AMC [air mobility command] forecast that we'll assign two crews to Turkey. It would be an intra-theater assignment flying from Turkey direct into Iraq, and then on to

Germany. I need solid nurses for this job. I need to know, if this tasking comes down, if you want to be on these crews?"

It was the kind of job that I'd always wanted and pushed for. I'd always felt that we needed to land as close to the battlefield as possible to quickly move the wounded to the regional hospital in Germany.

I told Jan, "I'll do my job in the CMC if needed. It's not the job I prefer. If a tactical assignment does come down, I want it. I know I'd do a good job."

The mission involved flying directly into the war zone to evacuate the wounded. There was a threat of triple-A (Anti-Aircraft Artillery) or SAMs (surface-to-air missiles). This was a new kind of mission for us since we converted to the C-17A Globemaster III. Many flyers did not understand the tactical mission. Most had spent their entire careers flying strategic missions on the forty-year-old C-141 jets. Strategic missions involved flying from a secure airfield in the rear to a safe airfield in Europe. There was no threat of being shot down.

I preferred the tactical mission because there were fewer hassles. The closer you flew to the front, the less paperwork and military crap you had to deal with. There was autonomy with aircrews and the ability to make independent decisions. On tactical missions, I felt in control, which made a difference in our patient's lives. Strategic missions were always controlled by Tanker Airlift Control Center (TACC).

TACC was at Scott AFB Illinois. You had to ask TACC for permission to do anything. Aircrews called it talking to MOTHER. There was no need for officers on the airplane, as far as I was concerned. TACC took away any decision-making on strategic missions.

# Citizen Call Up

February 23, 2003: *Hans Blix orders Iraq to destroy its Al Samoud 2 missiles by March 1st. The UN inspectors have determined that the missiles have an illegal range limit. Iraq can have missiles that reach neighboring countries, but not ones capable of reaching Israel. - CNN*

Since talking to Jan, rumors flew back and forth on who was going to be recalled to duty and when. Turkey was balking at having American troops in their country. The tactical mission I had hoped for faded. On February 23 orders finally arrived. The mobility officer called us in one at a time and briefed us.

"By direction of the President, you have been involuntarily recalled to active duty for a period of one year, with a possible extension to two. Your assignment is to serve as a flight nurse on a five-person crew."

I knew this was coming but was still shocked when Nate read the order. I assumed I would go back to the CMC when deploying to Turkey fell through. Nate saw the look on my face. "The commander and DO decided that you would serve on a crew and not in the CMC. If you don't like it, talk to them." I was happy. Someone else would have the thankless desk job while I got to fly.

The next day, our two crews and newly formed crew management cell were briefed on our mission. Jan presented us with an overview of the entire medical evacuation process.

We would base out of Mildenhall Air Base (AB) in England. From there we would fly to Sigonella, Sicily, and stage for medevac missions. When a tasking came down, we would launch from Sicily to Kuwait to pick up wounded and then fly direct to Ramstein AB in Germany. We would then return to England and start the loop over again. We were not permitted to fly over Turkish airspace, extending the flight time.

As the war developed, a navy fleet hospital would open in Spain. Patients would evacuate, alternating between Germany and Spain. Once Baghdad was secured, we would fly directly into Iraq to pick up the wounded.

I listened to the mission briefing and knew it wouldn't work. Jan asked if there were any questions. I said, "Who came up with this plan? The distances are too great. We'll bust duty days trying to fly that loop. This mission only works if everything occurs perfectly. We need to base out of Kuwait."

Jan stated, "That is what AMC had decided and we're stuck with it." It was not her plan; she was the messenger.

It was decided that we would not deploy as a whole squadron. The air evac system for the war was created piecemeal. Instead of flying with people I had worked with for years, we were fashioned into new provisional units. At one location, instead of having one trained squadron, we had a composite of ten different bases with ten different ideas on how to run operations. Who the hell thought this one up?

This instantly destroyed unit cohesiveness. The air force had training standards, but each home squadron had its individual personality and home court rules. Any *esprit de corps* was instantly destroyed when they stripped the stateside squadrons. This also split Jennifer and I up. She was assigned to another group and trained separately from me. Prior to deployment we saw little of each other.

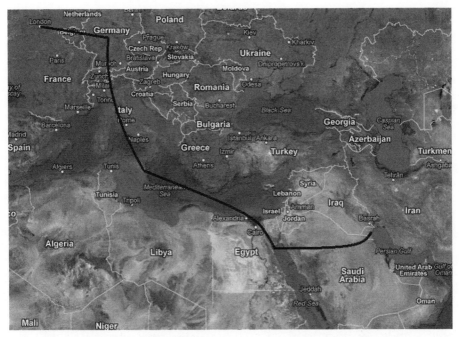

**Primary airevac route March 2003. Starting in England, transiting Germany and staging in Sicily. Casualties are recovered at Camp Wolf, Kuwait International Airport. (Google Maps 2013)**

The entire medical evacuation process was managed by TACC. I did not understand how evac missions from a war zone could be managed from Illinois. It added to the growing number of problems in the execution of the war.

Other omens presented during the buildup of forces. On active duty, we assumed that we would be treated like our full-time brothers. We reported to supply for our field gear issue. The sergeant directed us to bins loaded with musty green laundry bags. On the shelves I saw brand new, desert-issue gear, still in their wrappers. I asked, "Why aren't we getting the desert gear?"

"The desert equipment is for the active duty, and reservists get olive drab."

We opened the bags and found old Vietnam-era gear inside. Some of the webbing was rotted. Our Kevlar was not complete, and we had to cannibalize parts to make complete helmets.

The body armor did not come with ceramic chest plates, which had been designed specifically to stop a 7.62 millimeter rifle bullet—the primary bullet that the Iraqis used. When I asked where the plates were, I was told that they were too expensive and that we were not going to get them. Our body armor would only stop a nine millimeter handgun bullet. This was the ammo we carried for our pistols. In other words, my body armor would protect me if one of my crew accidentally shot me.

We were handed two tan flights suits and a desert jacket as charity.

This was not the supply sergeant's fault. Reservists were not funded as active duty. It was a two-tier system for money and equipment, though we were going to the same location and being exposed to the same risks.

The military did have smallpox and anthrax shots. The anthrax vaccine is highly controversial. My friend Dr. Buckley was court-martialed for refusing the shot. I knew pilots in our Wing that quit flying so they wouldn't have to take the shot.

We lined up for injections and were issued antibiotics and nerve agent antidotes. The Wing flight surgeon gave us a heart-to-heart talk, saying everything was safe. I thought about veterans of past generations who were exposed to nuclear testing, chemical weapons testing, DDT, and Agent Orange. They were also told it was safe. I wondered if twenty years from now I would be making a disability claim to the VA for some suppressed side affect from the vaccine. Like a good airman, I rolled up my sleeves and took both shots.

The anthrax shot burned into my deltoid and radiated out to my fingertips and across my shoulder. I had never experienced such pain from an injection before. A large welt, the size and color of an orange, formed on my arm. The rest of the day, I had difficulty holding a pen with my right hand.

My left arm leaked smallpox for a few days.

## March 7, 2003: *The intent of the Iraqi regime to keep from turning over all its weapons of mass destruction seems to me has not changed. - Colin Powell*

We were on-again, off-again for three weeks, and there was still no plane to take us overseas. I was tired of waiting and headed to Crystal Mountain to get one last day of skiing in. There was a late-season snowstorm and the skiing was epic. It was one of the few days in the Northwest where I was waist deep in powder. In the mid-afternoon, the clerk called my cell phone reporting we finally had transport.

By the time I got back to McChord, the plans had changed. We were to fly commercial to March Air Reserve Base (ARB) and then take a C-141 to England. I was frustrated with this decision. If we flew commercial, we would have to leave behind our ammunition, survival flares, smoke signals, and lithium batteries. We wouldn't be able to fly missions into the Middle East without this equipment. I griped that this was going to be a big mistake. No one would listen. I and other Desert Storm vets knew that if you did not leave home with it, you were never going to get it. I was told to shut up and get on the plane. Feelings that the medevac mission had been poorly planned just got worse.

Jennifer and I spent the night embraced in melancholy good-byes. Though trained for war, the actual act of saying good-bye was flushed with emotion and anxiety. There was no class or service manual to prepare us for the separation.

# Deployment

## 8 March, 2003

A long train of olive drab mobility bags followed us to the airport. It was the start of hauling everything we owned each time we were cattle-carted to a different country. The crews boarded an Alaskan Airlines flight to Riverside, California. Chief Master Sgt. Rick "Rock" Binkley was there to greet us. Rock used to be stationed at McChord. He transferred down to March after the C-141 was retired from Washington. We had history flying together. If I was on a plane in trouble, I would want Rock there. His vast knowledge of the C-141 and thousands of hours of flying convinced me that we could get through any in-flight emergency.

At first glance, Rock reminded me of an old-school marine gunny sergeant. In fact, the senior NCO was a former marine who crewed on helicopters. As soon as you met Rock, you recognized that he was a party. The chief had a family-style send-off at his house. Nurses, medics, and flight crew, toasting the unknown. The future was dark, and we didn't want to contemplate war. We drank until the beating war drums stopped pounding our heads.

Rick's house overlooked the desert valley of Riverside. We watched the sunset knowing we were involved in something bigger than all of us. Ribbons of daylight reflected on naive faces.

The next morning we reported to an outsized hangar that served as a troop holding area. We mingled with members of our expeditionary squadron, a hodgepodge of people from different bases. Immediately, I heard the phrase, "Well at our base, this is the way we did it." There was some animosity in the beginning, until we got to know one another. It would've been easier if command had not chopped the home squadrons.

The next three days are a vague memory with very little sleep. Any chance we could, we drank. After getting settled in England, I sent out the first of many e-mails to family and friends. Though I didn't realize it at the time, these e-mails became the genesis for the short stories that would develop into this book.

### Tuesday March 11, 2003

By direction of the President, Executive Order 13223D, my brother Eric and I have been recalled to active duty. We expect Jennifer to be recalled soon. Can't give any information on our mission or location until we arrive in-country. Troop movements are confidential.

I will try to send e-mail updates as much as possible. Please don't send any junk mail, jokes, or chain mail. Don't have the time.

I know there is a lot of concern about the validity of this war. I don't care to discuss it. I do ask that you support those of us who serve this country and defend it.

It took us over thirty-six hours to get overseas. Transiting four bases just to get to England. We are the first elements of our unit. There is plenty of work to be done to get the air evac system up and running. I'm disappointed how broken our airlift system is. The military is

working as usual. SNAFU is everywhere with long
lines for everything. Eat as much as you can at
each stop, unsure where the next meal is coming
from. Drink when you can, no ETOH downrange.

Morale is good, but not as high as Gulf War I.
Can't say I like seeing the protests on TV. But
I guess that is part of what I'm defending.
I'll check e-mail when I can. Supposed to be
computers at each station. Talk to you soon, I
hope.

I look forward to seeing my friends and the
mountains soon.

God bless America.

Ed 'RIV' Hrivnak, Captain, USAF

Aeromedical Evacuation Flight Nurse.

The arrival in England was a shock. I had expectations based from the first Gulf War. Desert Shield/Storm was efficient and well executed. This war lacked preparation and planning.

We arrived in England with nothing. No sleeping quarters; no building for the squadron to operate out of; no medical equipment, office supplies, or vehicles; and no funds to run the day-to-day operations. We had nurses, medics, and an inadequate support staff.

An advance party had arrived forty-eight hours prior. They accomplished purchasing discounted Harleys. Our initial briefing included Harley Davidson business cards while standing underneath an advertising banner. I had no idea who the commander was.

We organized into groups that focused on specific tasks for running an evac squadron. One group inventoried the trickling med supplies. Pallets arrived from war readiness stocks and were stacked outside. Millions of dollars worth of trauma equipment sat in the rain until we could find a condemned building to move into. This group dismantled pallets, listed each item, and then arranged them on makeshift shelves. Our first shelves consisted of old bleacher seats propped up on rotten wooden pallets.

Another party performed a detailed accounting of the narcotics and pharmacy. Control of narcotics was an ongoing problem. Morphine disappeared only to be found weeks later.

Another faction worked on establishing med resupply and stocking the actual kits that would be used on the wounded. There were no computers or modern tracking methods. Everything was done by hand on large yellow notepads.

My horde consisted of scroungers. Each day, the CMC made a list of critical items needed, which we would liberate. Brian, Tom, Jeremy, and I huddled, formulating a plan on how to find the needed paraphernalia.

We had no transportation and searched the base by walking. Then I located Rick, a friend stationed at Mildenhall. Rick was a combat controller, an elite profession that dealt with seizing airfields, directing airstrikes, and operating behind enemy lines. Though I had not seen him in four years, we picked up right where we left off. Military friendships work that way. Time and distance do not affect bonds of service.

Rick acquired a six-passenger truck with an open bed. We now had a means of transporting the equipment scrounged. Scrounging consisted of looking in dumpsters, searching the surplus yard for usable office equipment, and begging the Mildenhall air force personnel for handouts. We survived on charity the first month. We were homeless, dumpster diving.

There was a long list of items to acquire that included finding shelves to store our medical equipment, lockers for storing the pharmacy, liquid oxygen (LOX) for our patient oxygen system, a means of refilling emergency walk-around bottles, cleaning supplies, power cords, an inspections system for our medical equipment, and the hardest of all: the survival equipment and ammunition that we had left behind.

Quoting the life support sergeant at McChord, "Don't worry. Your equipment will be waiting for you overseas." I had known this was a lie.

The lack of survival equipment meant no active flying. We were stuck working ground support. My crew was trained to fly, so that's what we wanted to do. The lack of equipment became a personal vendetta for me. I didn't want to be grounded because of survival gear.

I called our home unit. They told me they were doing everything they could to get the stuff shipped. We worked and waited.

Our days were twelve to fourteen hours long and were spent organizing our makeshift squadron. The evenings involved driving to whatever quarters the CMC could find for us. Every few days, we moved to a new place to sleep. Some nights we slept in a five-star hotel. Some nights we slept in cots on the floor of the Mildenhall recreation building. We walked to the base gym, sharing showers with hundreds of other airmen that were kicked out of Turkey.

One of our first nights in English crew quarters involved a night of drinking and playing darts at the on-base pub. We were still getting to know each other and all felt a need to establish the strengths and weaknesses of each crewmember. Who could drink his fair share set a standard for others to follow. I noted early on that Jeremy could hold his liquor, while I established the reputation of being a cheap date. I had a buzz going after only two drinks.

Jeremy had worked with me in the Reserves, but we didn't know each other well. He had a name as a squared-away NCO. I sized him up while we drank. He was a tall, proud Makah American Indian from the northwestern tip of Washington State. He had a dark complexion and hair that was cut razor sharp into a flattop. He rarely smiled unless he trusted you. He preferred silence and a professional stance until he had a drink. Then his wit and unusual humor took over. We would end up spending our entire deployment together.

It was understood that no matter how much you drank, you were ready for duty in the morning, even if it was an early alert.

The following dawn we were standing on the street corner waiting for a military bus to take us to Mildenhall. The troops had assembled, but no Jeremy. Tom, Brian, and I all thought the same thing: Jeremy had drank too much and slept past or forgot to set an alarm. There was no time to waste.

I held the bus while Tom and Brian ran to Jeremy's room. They reached the front door and pounded loudly.

No response.

They pounded again and yelled for Jeremy. Tom listened closely. Even with hearing loss from years of flying, Tom thought he heard a noise. Very faintly he heard a quiet tapping. Three short taps, three long taps, and three short taps. Tom could not believe what he had heard. He pounded again and listened. Jeremy was tapping the international Morse code for distress: SOS. Tom and Brian looked at each other and feared the worst. Jeremy could have slipped in the shower and broken his leg. Any number of things could have happened during his drunken walk back to quarters.

Brian came back around to the bus stop just as I was leaving to find them. The bus had arrived and I was not sure how long I could stall. Brian explained the SOS. We ran back to the building, looking for a master key. We found the cleaning lady, who let us into the room. We opened the door and there was no Jeremy. Jeremy's bags were packed, his uniform was out, and there was a smell of air freshener in the room. Jeremy was disabled in the bathroom.

We opened the bathroom door, expecting to find a bloody and disfigured body. Instead, there was Jeremy, standing in his underwear with his dog tags in his hands. The bathroom reeked of air freshener and the door lock was partially disassembled. There was no time for an explanation. We needed to catch the bus. Jeremy collected his uniform and pack, and we ran for the bus. On the drive to Mildenhall, we got the whole story.

Jeremy woke as scheduled to do his morning routine. He made some coffee and went into the shower. The bathroom is shared, so it can be locked from the outside. Unknown to Jeremy, the bathroom door locked behind him on this fateful morning. He finished his shower and grabbed the door. As soon as he grabbed the locked door handle, he realized he was *locked in* the bathroom.

He knew the consequences of being late for the bus: he would have to buy drinks for everyone that night. Jeremy immediately went into James Bond mode.

First he tried yelling and pounding on his neighbor's door for help. No luck—no one was next door. He then grabbed the air freshener and sprayed it into the smoke detector, hoping to set off the fire alarm. Setting off the fire alarm, evacuating the building, and having the fire department arrive would be far less damaging than having to buy drinks for everyone that night. The fire alarm didn't sound. Jeremy knew he was running out of time.

He then grabbed his dog tags from around his neck and used one as a tool to try and disassemble the door lock. He managed to get inside the lock but could not free the locking mechanism. Jeremy was working on the lock when Tom and Brian knocked on the outside door. They couldn't hear Jeremy yell for help, but they could hear Jeremy knocking SOS. Luckily for Jeremy, Tom was previously enlisted in the army and recognized Morse code (almost no one in the modern military learns Morse code).

That night Jeremy bought the drinks at the pub and was given the nickname "Loo," the British slang for bathroom.

The four of us were inseparable in our off time. We trained together prior to shipping out and drank together overseas. Tom was the senior officer of our crew, with the rank of Major. He came up through the ranks—an enlisted mustang, which means he has more going for him than many officers. Having shared experiences of basic training, enlisted life in the barracks, KP (kitchen patrol), and guard duty provides a unique perspective to mustangs.

Tom was a nurse practitioner in Washington, bringing a wealth of knowledge to the team. He was the stabilizing force of our crew, letting us have the fun we wanted, but not pushing it to where we ended up in a navy brig or army stockade. Tom's professionalism gave our crew comfort, knowing he was not going to get us killed or let us kill a patient. He was our safety net. His balding head, graying hair, and crow's-feet spoke of experience, not age.

Brian and I had a multitude of past experiences together. We whored around together when we were single. Some wondered if we would ever get married as much as we had enjoyed bachelor life. Two good women did settle us down. Brian was a dashing firefighter back in Washington. Slicked back black hair, flashing smile, and ease with conversation let Brian move effortlessly within in a bar. When we got together, we talked like we were still single, knowing who we answered to when we got home.

Brain was later assigned to another crew, yet our paths crossed many times during the war. The four of us managed to get together in different countries. Even today, there is a connection between the four of us. A few days after the bathroom accident, we were given a day off. Jeremy, Tom, Brian, and I rode the tube to downtown London.

We had a few hours and tried to see what London had to offer. We saw the sights of Trafalgar Square and Piccadilly Circus, with a quick pint or two at pubs with fish and chips. We were American airmen doing the same thing the Greatest Generation experienced in World War II. We watched the changing of the guards. We were lucky enough to see the war veterans of the Irish Guards march for Saint Patrick's Day.

These old men wore crisp, dark suits with top hats. Adorning their jackets were medals from historic battle, and their cadence in perfect step, with chins held high. As they marched by, I stood at attention and saluted. They passed in review with heads locked forward, except for one old gentleman who turned his eyes towards me. He recognized that I saluted as an American. My high and tight haircut was a giveaway for military. He looked at me with the knowledge of a man who had seen too much war. He gave me a nod that said, "It's your turn, Sonny."

One of our last stops was the Imperial War Museum. It was depressing. The war museum impressed on us that all of human history has been plagued by war. We've had more years of war than of peace. I thought about how there are no museums that preserve the history of peace.

One of the exhibits I went through was "the London Blitz." It was underground and gave a feeling of life in London during the German air raids. You started out sitting tightly packed in a bunker and went though a simulated bombing. Voices were dubbed in of children crying and adults calming each other. After that, our tour group walked though a bombed-out section of London. I tripped over a leaking fire hose. I could smell burnt wood. Kids' toys were scattered among the rubble. Voices were dubbed in of family searching for loved ones. The exhibit was chilling. It gave me a vivid reminder of the ruined buildings of the Oklahoma City Bombing (I had responded there with an urban rescue team looking for survivors in April 1995). The exhibit made me sick. I guess that was its intention. I walked out of the museum pondering human history. Why do we fight? What were we about to do?

I left the museum and waited for my friends with little time left to catch the tube back to our quarters. As sure as Bob's your uncle, we made sure to have another pint before returning to base.

We sensed the war was close. Our workdays were getting longer as we readied the squadron for combat operations. We consolidated our personal equipment and prepared for weeks on the road.

An evening after a full day of ground support and drinks, Tom decided to shine his combat boots. I watched with mild interest and sipped a martini. Tom placed a lighter under the can of shoe polish to warm it up. He gave me a running commentary on the finer points of spit shining. I listened like a hung-over freshman college student.

Without warning, the can of wax burst into flames. I stared with amusement unmoved, wondered what would happen next. Tom lunged with the burning can and ran for the bathroom. As he ran, flaming wax splashed from the can and lit the carpet on fire. I sat down my martini and decided this was out of hand, grabbed one of my combat boots and stomped out the flames. I followed the blazing trail into the bathroom, rounding the corner in time to hear Tom yelp. He had placed the burning can of wax in the sink and turned the water on. The molten wax splattered throughout the room, covering the white sink, walls, mirror, and Tom's hand with black wax. Tom suffered second-degree burns to several of his fingers. The bathroom was trashed. Tom cleaned and dressed his wounds while I made sure all the fires were out. He then called the front desk to inform them we had had an accident. Two Pakistani men arrived and cleaned the room. They never asked what happened and simply smiled. Tom had to wear gloves to hide his wounds from the rest of the squadron. Burns on the hands would have grounded him.

As the war loomed, the English protested the war. A demonstrator breeched the fence line and biked naked down the runway. The air force's response was swift. Anyone not actively flying performed guard duty. We formed into squads and went in shifts to guard the aircraft. We had no weapons. The security police (SPs) gave us a two- way radio with a dead battery and an air horn to sound if we were attacked. All I needed was a red rubber nose and clown shoes. It was a knee-jerk reaction and we were completely ineffective to stop naked bikers.

I had performed guard duty before, when I was enlisted. Guard duty has not changed with time. It was painfully boring with hours of staring at the flight line, trying to keep the brain active and the body warm. The cold winter had set in and we had a few days of freezing rain. The aircraft mechanics took pity as they laughed and provided us with heaters. The SPs delivered pizza. We took turns walking to the hangar to call our wives on the DSN (military phone) and grab a cup of coffee.

I was able to talk with Jennifer briefly. She was shipping out soon for Oman to fly tactical evac on smaller C-130 transports. It was one of the few times I heard from her during the deployment. She had little opportunity to e-mail or call. Jennifer, my love of four years, became a phantom of our past lives.

# March 17, 2003

I was ordered to perform round-robin flights to the hub bases, evaluating if we were ready for war. I flew with the chief of the squadron. We had jump orders granting permission to hop on any military transport aircraft. We didn't work together and had our own agendas. I had a poor first impression of the chief. He was one of the advance party that had bought a new motorcycle.

Where was this chief coming from? What was his purpose in the squadron? I rarely saw him on the flight line where the physical work was accomplished.

The first stop was Sigonella AB, Sicily. The island was a garden spot for our jump-off point to the war. It was a haven that we would cherish prior to facing wounded.

I was surprised at the lack of preparation. We were tasked to launch up to three medevac missions a day. Due to a lack of personnel, equipment, and spare parts, I surmised we could handle a single C-141 mission a day. I give credit to the operations team in Sicily. They were making the best of a difficult situation. Adversity was inspiring their morale. They worked long days, with little time off. They were proud of what they were doing and tackling the challenge.

We stayed in Sicily just long enough for briefings by the key officers and senior NCOs. We slept a few hours in the hangar and then went on to Spain.

Spain was home of deployed Fleet Hospital 8. They had built an inflatable hospital and had already handled a few noncombat evac missions. They did this without the help of an air force mobile aeromedical staging flight (MASF) or aeromedical evacuation operations team (AEOT).

I went to the air ops center expecting to be briefed by the navy. Instead, fourteen senior officers and NCOs marched in the room wanting answers on the air force air evac system. I was caught off guard. The commander of naval air operations for the base asked me, "Just what the hell is the air force's plan?" He and I locked eyes. I realized that this man was a serious, professional aviator. He was the naval officer from the old school of polished brass and crisp white uniforms. I knew from his look that he was not a man to bullshit.

Standing up front, I scrapped together an overview of the evac plan. I was nervous. I had no prepared presentation. The navy was not impressed with the air force. The ops officer kept glaring. He had a right to. The air force had not done its job and a low-ranking captain represented poorly. There were several unanswered questions to arise out of the meeting.

During surge operations, we were required to move three fully loaded C-141 aircraft a day from the Gulf to Germany and Spain. A configured C-141 consisted of eighty to ninety patients. The fleet hospital could safely handle over a hundred patients a day if there was a means of moving them stateside. The stateside plan called for converted 767 jetliners to move the patients to the States. A specially made patient loading system (PLS) was needed to lift the patients into the 767 airplane door. The problem was that there was no PLS at Spain, and only limited ramp space for the evac aircraft. There was room on the ramp for one heavy jet, provided that none of the planes broke.

I instilled the idea to prepare for the worst-case scenario. Was there a plan in place if a plane broke? (No.) Was there in-route maintenance to service C-141 and 767 aircraft? (No.) Was there any plan for multiple in-flight fatalities? (No, the morgue could only handle one body.) Was there any decontamination (DECON) equipment in case a wounded soldier slipped by with a biological or chemical exposure? (No, it was assumed that all patients would be completely DECON'd in the Middle East.) Was there a way to provide meals to the patients flying stateside? (No.)

These holes were not the responsibility of the navy. The air force should have been handling the details. Pieces of the plan were in place, but we were not ready for surge operations. I felt that Spain could safely handle one mission a day out of the Middle East. This was provided that there were less than a hundred casualties a day and few in-flight deaths. This was also assuming there were no chemical and biological weapons.

An AEOT and MASF were to be deployed to support the navy. There was a shortage of airlift to get them in place. They were still stateside. The AEOT's job was to coordinate the medical evacuation. This included medical supplies, configuring the aircraft, managing the flight nurses and medics, and monitoring the flow of evac aircraft in and out of Spain.

The MASF did the physical hands-on work of the patient transfer. They loaded and unloaded the wounded. They transferred the patients to the fleet hospital and prepared them for flights stateside. The meeting produced a punch list to work on and dissatisfied naval officers.

While in Spain, I tried to scam survival equipment. I went from survival shop to survival shop talking it up about supporting the war effort. It didn't work. The navy was not impressed by the petty skills of an air force con artist. They were polite with me but not about to help a boy in blue.

# The American
# Invasion of Iraq

March 20, 2003 *The War on Iraqi begins. Two F-117s carrying two 2,000-pound bombs a piece struck the suspected bunker of Saddam Hussein. -CNN*

The war started for me while watching CNN. I was having a gin and tonic at the Rota club. I witnessed the "Shock and Awe" from a barstool. I felt the need to get back to England. Not that there was a rush for my crew. We still had no survival equipment. Other crews in the squadron were now pulling alert duty and flying evac missions. My group of scroungers was stuck on the ground.

I searched for a ride back, and the air ops commander offered a flight to Mildenhall in the base commander's C-12. The C-12 is a small, twin-engine turboprop plane used for light transport. The plane was slow, but it was a nonstop flight. I readily accepted. The chief of our squadron elected to fly a different mission via Germany. He said he had some "business" there to take care of. I suspected the business had something to do with motorcycles.

## March 22, 2003 *Two US marines killed in Southern Iraq. First combat related casualties of the war.* -*CNN*

When I reported to the C-12, the air ops officer asked me if I had any luck pilfering survival equipment. I smiled sheepishly. He told me it was his job to know everything that happened on his flight line, including an air force officer trying to steal survival equipment. I had been caught, but he left it at that.

Flying back over the white cliffs of Dover, I had no sense of relief like aircrews of past wars. My war had just started. England was clear that day, not the normal dreary wet countryside. The rolling fields did not invite; I wanted out of England to attack our mission.

I wasted no time on survival gear, resorting to the time-honored method of military supply: bartering. I traded three cases of beer and seven nine millimeter Beretta magazines with the survival shop sergeant and the SP armorer. We had our bullets, flares, and batteries.

While waiting to be assigned a mission, our crew assisted with launching aircraft. One day I ran a forklift. The next day I might pack med kits with trauma bandages and IV supplies. Then we would recover crews coming back from the Middle East.

Our life in England changed. No one complained that we were outcasts from Turkey. Crews worked sixteen-hour days with a purpose. We no longer had any downtime. There was no time to guard planes from naked bikers. The noise on the flight line was deafening. War machines launching at regular intervals: tankers, transports, bombers, and fighters. It was impressive to watch, and I was proud to be a part of it.

I looked around and saw reservists in their fifties with gray hair. They didn't need to be there. Many of them had over twenty years in and could have retired. They were back for another war, doing their part as citizen airmen. We were short on staffing, equipment, and planes. We were tired, yet morale was good. I swelled with pride. No one was willing to give up. Though our days were long, our work and living conditions were easy compared to the GIs in the field and the damaged humans that arrived by stretcher.

The tempo of the mission picked up. We started with three missions a week, then one a day, and then sometimes twice a day. The magnitude was overwhelming. We relearned medevac. The military had not endured casualties like that since the Vietnam War. I would have rather been learning than been a seasoned pro.

The fog of war was very much alive. Little went right, yet we made positive progress every day. Communication was an effort. It was challenging to talk to the army, navy, and sometimes even our own air force.

I was glad I was there. Was it for God and country? To win one for the Gipper? To free Iraq? I don't know. My friends were there, and I'd have felt guilty if I hadn't endured it and helped my wounded brothers. The uniform was and is a strong attachment.

After living in England for three weeks, I finally met the squadron commander. He was a short, overweight man wearing Radar O'Reilly glasses. He spent too many years flying a desk. I gave him a written report on our readiness status. He wasn't pleased with the report. I stated that we weren't prepared for extended combat operations. The lack of spare parts, personnel, and planes would keep us from surging to three missions a day. He told me he was not going to submit my report but only use portions of it in his own report. In other words, he did not want higher command to know how ill equipped we were for war. I left his office knowing he would not transmit such a blunt, honest assessment. I wish I had kept a copy of it. I'm sure it's sitting in an English landfill.

## March 28, 2003 *Twelve marines are listed as missing in action in vicinity of Nasiriya. -CNN*

I was assigned to a crew as Medical Crew Director (MCD). I replaced an MCD that was relieved of duty for missing a flight back to England.

Not his fault, but he was in command and ultimately blamed for it. I was responsible for a crew and the safe transport of wounded. I was handed part of a crew that has already flown one evac mission. They filled me in on what to expect. The relieved director, Mark, provided details: "Expect multiple missile attacks. We had several while there. It was a chore running wounded from the plane to the bunkers. We had to gas mask patients that could not help themselves. We finally decided to load the patients and get out of there. It's taking too long running back and forth from the bunkers."

These first days of war carried uncertainty. Many of us were convinced that the Iraqis were going to use chemical and biological weapons. Precautions were taken in the months of March and April to protect against incoming missiles. The Scuds and short-range missiles that the Iraqis used were not very accurate, but no one wanted to get hit by a lucky missile loaded with mustard gas or anthrax. I knew what a conventional missile could do and imagined that a chemical or biological weapon would be devastating.

(During the first Gulf War, I had gone through a Scud attack in Riyadh, Saudi Arabia. The missile didn't come close to hitting us. I sent a letter to my father stating that the Iraqis could not hit the side of an airport with one of those missiles. A few days later, a conventional Scud struck Dhahran, Saudi Arabia. Twenty-nine soldiers were dead and ninety-nine were wounded, decimating an Army Reserve unit from Greensburg, PA. I stopped boasting).

I had Brian from my original crew, along with crew that had each completed one mission. We landed at Sigonella, Sicily, where the aeromedical crews were expanded to seven to accommodate the twenty four hour duty day. I noticed on the status board that Tom's crew was short people and I volunteered the two of us for transfer over—although Tom needed two nurses and Brian is a medic. They split us. Brain gave me the stink eye as the CMC reassigned me to Tom's crew. To this day, Brian rides me about leaving him behind. He refuses to forgive me, though he tells me he would have done the same. I made a mistake.

I saw that Jeremy was on Tom's crew, but I didn't recognize the other names.

# First Mission

March 31, 2003 *UK marines push on for Basra-Relentless strikes hit Baghdad. -CNN*

We were alerted for our first mission. I arrived at the hangar and met the crew for the first time. I was glad to see my friends, Tom and Jeremy. It was time to size up the rest of the crew.

Lieutenant Cathleen Likens was older than me. She didn't stand when I introduced myself. She was petite and quiet. Could she lift a litter? My first impression was doubt that she would fit in. She was from Washington, DC, and provided little information about herself. I prejudged that she was too timid for this kind of work.

We worked together checking our med kits. We had a thousand pounds of equipment to load onto the jet by hand. In walked Staff Sgt. Jimmy Natio. He was immediately barking orders on how to load the equipment. First impression: Jimmy was a pushy little man. Jimmy knew his job and was self-confident. He knew efficient ways to load, secure, and work with the medical equipment. I learned to trust his judgment. Born of Japanese blood, single Sgt. Natio added culture to our crew. Jimmy was a substitute teacher and repaired bicycles in civilian life. He was preparing to become an air force pilot in California. After the medical equipment was loaded in the van, we signed out narcotics and weapons.

Technical Sgt. Steve Nunez was our weapons courier. He carried the nine millimeter Berretta handguns and extra ammunition. We talked about handling weapons. In the past, medevac crews didn't carry weapons. This was a different kind of war. The War on Terrorism had no front lines. There were no safe areas. Any American, especially one in uniform, was a target. We agreed that weapons would be handed out during the combat entry checklist. Magazines were loaded, but rounds would not be chambered in the barrel. I suggested that anyone not proficient with a weapon should leave the guns in the gun box. Medicos were notorious for being sloppy with weapons. I watched Steve handle the Beretta. He was safe and meticulous.

Sgt. Nunez was a proud Hispanic. Back home, he was a mental health counselor, married with children in California. He was a voice of reason on our crew, rarely raising his voice.

We then moved to the intel briefing.

Intelligence detailed the area to which we were flying. The briefing explained the threat level, how many missiles were fired, whether planes were hit, and what to expect when landing in-country. We were shown satellite photos of the airfield, clearly seeing both where we would park and the location of the closest bunkers. We were briefed on the available combat search and rescue (CSAR) forces and the codes for the day. We also reviewed our ISOPREP cards. These cards had personal information that would be used by CSAR to identify shot down aircrew.

Next was the patient report. This report consisted of how many patients there were, the types of injuries, and where we'd take our patients. After this mission, we learned that the number of patients often doubled by the time we landed. It was eight hours from briefing to when we were actually in-country. The briefer told us to expect ten combat casualties. Two of the patients were priority patients. They needed advanced care within forty-eight hours of injury. Their clock had started hours prior.

I looked at the evac crew during the briefing. I saw no looks of fear or concern. The crew was focused on the mission. Tom made eye contact with me. He was in command. He too was evaluating. We both weighed how we would perform with this untested crew.

When I recall all the missions I've flown in my career, I remember the briefing and feelings of our first combat mission. It's how a football team feels reaching the Super Bowl. We'd spent years training and preparing for this very moment. Now it was time for the main event. But this wasn't a game. It was not a routine peacetime mission or a training mission. The patients were not mannequins. They weren't stable retirees or spouses flying back to the States to have babies. We were en route to an inhospitable desert to fly out combat wounded and mistakes could be deadly. After our briefings and schedule delays, we headed to the jet.

At the plane was my first chance to talk to our fourth medic. Technical Sgt. Robert Beraras had dark skin and was sweating a waterfall off his forehead from the stifling Sicilian air. His smile was warm and jovial to match his weight. He was laughing.

The plane was loaded with cargo, and there was little room. Robert was laughing about how squeezed we were. We had to force our equipment through a tiny escape hatch on the side of the plane. I immediately liked Robert. He laughed at adversity. Robert's positive attitude was infectious with the rest of the crew. During tense moments, Robert would talk in East L.A. Hispanic slang. Robert was also a native of California and friends with Steve. On the outside, he was a health inspector.

I asked the crew chief why the plane was loaded with cargo. There were supposed to be a dozen C-141 aircraft committed for medical evac. The chief told me, "That's true, but there aren't enough transports for all the cargo. We're ordered to load the planes with cargo unless it's an urgent, short-notice mission."

We would configure the aircraft on the ground in Kuwait. This would extend our ground time, thus exposing us. Short ground times were key to survival. A plane parked on the ramp too long became a target. There was also a steady, never-ending stream of jets behind us wanting to park in our spot. The loadmasters and engineers buttoned the plane for take off.

We milled about and waited for another clearance delay. Many of the countries we flew over were not happy about the Iraq War. Diplomatic clearance was a dance with foreign officials. Our alert started at 9:00 a.m. It was now late at night, we were tired, and we hadn't started treating wounded. We exchanged small talk and continued the size-up. I was not excited about our first mission with a crew I didn't know. Learning some facts about them eased my fears.

The seven of us combined had over one hundred years of military service and 8,300 flight hours. The crew had extensive civilian medical experience and knowledge. Our four medics spoke Spanish, Japanese, some Makah, and enough German to order beers and dinner. We were from three different parts of the US and four diverse cultures.

Could we handle this? I again looked at Cathleen and prejudged. She was the only woman on our crew. She was hushed and worked with a purpose.

The APU (auxiliary power unit) finally fired off, and the jet engines started in sequence. I listened on the headset as the front-end crew brought the old girl to life. The C-141 was a tired, war-weary plane. Built in the sixties, she was on her last mission. After the war, the remaining twelve aircraft we flew would be sent to the bone yard and dismembered. The reservists from California that operated the jet expertly fixed the glitches we had experienced on start-up. For most of them, this would also be their last war. They, along with the plane had survived Vietnam, Grenada, Panama, Desert Storm, Bosnia, Somalia, Rwanda, and countless unnamed brush-fire wars and humanitarian missions.

The crew hatch was sealed shut and the jet was pressurized. Creaking and grinding reverberated as the brakes released and the wheels clawed the tarmac to move the beast. She was heavily laden with fuel, cargo, and human life. I looked outside one last time, searching for Mt. Etna. There was no moon to expose the snow-capped volcano that rose majestically over the Sicilian countryside.

We scanned the cabin, looking for a place to nap. Once airborne, the crew scrambled to stretch out. I lay my poncho liner on top of a cargo pallet and tried to nap.

I was now nervous. Would there be Scud attacks? Would I be able to handle the wounded? It wasn't an ER. There was only seven of us to care for patients. We had no doctor or support services. For eight to ten hours, we were it. I dozed off for, at most, two hours. I dreamt of fear. When I awoke, things began happening quickly.

We were entering the AOR (area of responsibility), better known as the "war zone," "downrange," "the sand box," or simply "the box." Word was passed through the intercom that there was no room to land in Kuwait. The field was MOGged out (military aircraft on ground). No place to park.

An hour and a half prior to landing, we readied. We donned our gear: nine millimeter Beretta, sixty rounds of ammo, body armor, gas mask, Kevlar helmet, and field gear. Laid next to me were a chemical/biological suit and a survival vest. Most sat on their flak vests. There was also pro gear: the quick-don oxygen mask, Camelbak, walk-around bottle, checklist, dog tags, Nomex gloves, latex gloves, pocket mask, eye protection, and our medical kit.

The flight engineer mechanically and calmly recited the combat entry checklist. The pilots pitched the plane over, diving for the ground. Loose debris slid forward in the cargo hold. An abandoned cold cup of coffee slapped against the bulkhead. We in the back held onto our web seats and gear.

The loadmasters armed defensive systems and manned the back doors. They peered outside, looking for SAMs (surface-to-air missiles) and small arms fire. Both held a toggle switch to launch flares, a tactic designed to defeat the heat seeking missiles. Below ten thousand feet, the aircraft was depressurized. That way a hole shot through the plane would not cause an explosive decompression. You knew the plane was depressurized because you could smell the Middle East. The smell had a hint of heated garbage. The air sweltered. During all of this, we ate and drank as much as we could tolerate. We spread out in the aircraft to minimize being hit by the same ground fire. Spreading out was not practical. The plane was so burdened with cargo; we were squeezed in a tiny compartment.

The pilots flew a random pattern to minimize the target. Depending on the pilot, the winds, and the heat of the day, the approach could be nauseating. By the time the plane contacted the earth, sweat glands were working overtime.

Land. Immediately out of seats and getting ready for patients. The loadmasters disarmed the flares. We flew down with beans and bullets and now reconfigured the aircraft for wounded, moving as much as we could. There was no room to park. The field was MOGged, and we waited an hour for parking. Ground personnel were spotted. The only gear worn were the chem masks stored on the hips. The airfield was cold and no Scuds. Saddam was not supposed to have any Scud missiles, though dozens had already struck. We stripped gear, keeping weapons and masks handy.

The cargo hold was dark, and condensation dripped from air-conditioning attempting to keep up with the desert heat. Kuwait International airport was surprisingly humid for a sandy wasteland. The loads unpinned the pressure door and opened the large clamshell that would eject our cargo and embrace the wounded. As the ass end of our home opened, the weight of the desert insulted our bodies with force. The light temporarily blinded us as desert debris invaded our flying hospital. The sand was alive and swirled into the crevices and cracks of both the plane and our skin. Like 9/11, this was a crucial moment. My thirty-three years of living and sixteen years of military service came down to this. All my training and life experience was now weighed against the trauma of combat. This was my ultimate test.

In the distance, I saw a shimmering parade of Humvee ambulances and am-buses.

*Our patients had arrived.*

The patient load was 11-7+2 and a duty passenger. That meant eleven litter patients, seven walking wounded, and two attendants. Some took care of themselves, some needed lots of help. All had been waiting for us for a long time and needed pain medicine and antibiotics. The injuries to the patients included: gun shot wounds (GSW) to the stomach, partial amputations from land mines, open fractures secondary to GSW, head injury/struck by a tank, blast injuries, shrapnel injuries, and dislocations. The patients were mainly from the marines and 101st Airborne Screaming Eagles. Many were involved in ambushes. There were a spattering of noncombat injuries and medical patients.

We loaded patients without delay. I asked the ground medics if they would like beer on our next run. They would rather have had more litters. The litters go out on the plane but rarely make it back. One of our litters was broken and is jerry-rigged.

The aircrew started engines while we donned our armor and Kevlar. Everything was fast-paced, getting the patients ready for takeoff. The nurses pushed morphine to get the GIs comfortable. We ended up having a five-hour ground time. Take-off was uneventful. The aircraft remained unpressurized until it could climb above any potential threats. The loadmasters stood in the troop doors and manned the flares until we were out of SAM range.

For the next eight and a half hours, it was intense nursing. The wounded were behind on medications. I had a chest tube that gave me fits for the most of the flight, forced to constantly adjust the suction to keep the patient comfortable. I suspected there was a small leak, and air was filling outside the lung, creating a pneumothorax. The wounds were dirty, and the patients required multiple antibiotics. One GI was already infected and spiked a fever. Another patient passed out from dehydration and required fluid resuscitation. We ran low on IV tubing, gloves, and alcohol wipes. I was the Good Humor man and handed out morphine like candy.

We dealt with the post-traumatic stress of combat. When possible, we talked with the wounded to assess their well-being. (In the civilian ER, I rarely did this.) One trooper confided in me that he witnessed Iraqi children run over by a convoy. He was in the convoy, and they had strict orders not to stop. If a vehicle stopped, it was an isolated and an inviting target for RPGs (rocket-propelled grenades). He told me that women and children had been forced out onto the road to break up the convoy so the Iraqi irregulars could get a clear shot. He told me that dealing with that sight was worse than the pain of his injury. The convoys did not stop.

The marine with the belly wound had a purple heart pinned to his pillow. I asked him if the medal meant anything to him. He stated, "Maybe some day, when I am older and out of this mess, it may mean something. Today, my stomach hurts and I'm spending time in the hospital." He was a quiet, humble, reserved marine, and I was privileged to care for him. He represented the best of the military and our country. I attempted to give him and the casualties the best care possible.

A GI with shrapnel wounds was angry at being ambushed. "We lost most of our Humvees to mortar fire. Many were wounded in the ambush. . . . There was metal flying everywhere, but luckily no one was killed."

The GI with the amputation stared at the litter above him. We talked about his wounds. "This sucks, but I'm lucky to be alive . . . I'm glad I'm still alive." My knees protested as I struggled to stand up from the floor.

The C-141 was not a hospital. The plane was loud and poorly lit. We stacked the patients three to four high in the litter stanchions. A headlamp was needed to see patients on the bottom. The plane was fairly dirty. We rarely performed wound care on the plane, packing another dressing on top of a leaking wound. It's not a sterile environment. Fluid bled overhead from aging hydraulic lines. Condensation from the ventilation system caused water to drip in places. There were hot and cold spots in the airplane. You had to watch where you loaded patients because of overhead blowers. It was a large human dehydrator. The pressurization system drew moisture out of the air. Plus we had very little moisture cruising at thirty-five thousand feet. Patients that required IV fluids needed more because of the dehydrating effect. The rhythm and the vibration of the plane were fatiguing. The oxygen partial pressure at altitude is less than at sea level. (An inflated balloon expanded in flight because of the lack of pressure. It would collapse when descending as pressure increased.) Though not aware of it, healthy passengers breathed faster in an eight thousand-foot cabin altitude. This dehydrated them faster as they exhaled the moisture. After ten hours of flying in this environment, we landed utterly exhausted. However we felt, think how the patient with the gunshot wound to the chest felt, laying there wrapped in dressings unable to move.

Somehow, each of the crew managed a forty-five minute break to slam down some MREs and catch a thirty-minute power nap. We landed at Germany in the middle of the night. Film clips seen on TV were of our squadron bringing patients back. No media for us. It was too late, cold, and dark for the media. It was fine. News cameras were a distraction and hampered unloading.

The patients were off-loaded, and we cleaned up the mess. Used bandages, IV tubing, and needles were picked off the cargo floor. Heart monitors, suctions, and pumps were packed. Then a sergeant arrived and ordered us to sign papers stating we would not drink and drive in Germany. We were pissed. Our mission from start to finish was twenty-nine hours long. Most of us were up twelve hours prior to that, minus catnaps. Forty-one hours later and staff was worried we might drink and drive. We had no cars! Apparently, drinking after a mission had already become a problem.

Kuwait came under rocket attack after we left. We had a cold airfield and considered ourselves lucky.

Though later missions would be longer with more casualties, it was that first mission that was defining for me, because of the unknown. Because we were untested. It was the Olympic trials. That one mission was the high-water mark of my air force career. We succeeded. No one shot at us, and everyone lived. A very simple equation. It was the most rewarding because it was the most challenging. A lifetime of preparation paid off.

## April 1, 2003: *A Patriot missile battery shoots down an Iraqi missile before it reaches Kuwait. -CNN*

# Sembach Air Base, Germany

I woke with vague recollection, got out of bed, and opened the curtains and window. The clear sunshine burned my eyes and caused a headache. My eyes adjusted to see rolling fertile hills and a German fighter jet flying low in the valley before me. Deep breath in. The hallmark of life.

I looked inside the room. Empty beer bottles and flight gear were strewn about. I stank from the mission, failing to shower before bed. I dressed to run and clear my head.

While jogging, I recalled the events of the night. We were on the tarmac in Germany for a long time, waiting for the ambuses to show up. There was confusion at Ramstein AB. We passed off the wounded, cleaned the cargo floor, and waited for a ride to take us to sleep. What to do with us? No one would take ownership. We made it to the lodging office only to be told there was no room in the inn. We sat drinking beer and watching the porn channel on German TV. The crew joked about the porn soon to be viewed in our rooms.

"Do we get private rooms?" Jeremy asked.

"I hope so," I responded with a superficial smile.

Someone found rooms at Sembach, forty-five minutes away. No one cared. We were too tired. I bought more beer for the road trip and passed them out. I recalled the no drinking and driving rule. It didn't apply to buses. Staff was more concerned about filling out the right forms instead of us getting some overdue sleep.

There was little talk during the bus ride. We found our rooms around 3:00 a.m. Tom and Jeremy came up to finish the beer. I recalled intense exhaustion, the sense that my spirit was completely sapped. I was a rubber band that has been stretched but hadn't snapped. Sleep and exercise helped the band to retain its shape.

Cathleen calling my name brought me back both to the present and to my run.

I came to a stop so I could talk to Cathleen Likens. She had tired eyes. A shower and fresh civilian clothes did wonders for the rest of her. She was fit, and her eyes were the only things that looked worn out. My eyes must have looked the same. She reminded me that the crew was meeting at the all ranks club. I ran off to shower and made it in time for brunch.

At brunch, the crew debriefed the mission. It was lighthearted. Cathleen was the last one to show. She stood before us and said, "I just saw the AC [aircraft commander]. He said the plane's broke and we have another twenty-four hours off."

The crew broke into cheers. Tired faces beamed at Cathleen. We looked up to her, hopeful she had more to add. There was a pause. She smiled and delivered the not-so-obvious "April fools."

Shoulders slumped. We forgot it was April 1. From that point on, Cathleen was out of her shell and engaged with the crew. She was not the quiet nurse that I doubted. She had just needed time to learn how to navigate six male egos. During brunch, I learned that she was a family practice nurse and had served twenty-one years in the military. Lt. Likens, like Tom and I, came up through the ranks before being commissioned as an officer. It was exceptionally rare to have three mustangs on one crew.

Cathleen was a hard working provider on the plane who rarely complained and stayed focused on treating the wounded. I hardly saw her take a break. She was always at someone's side.

The debrief began. We were satisfied with crew performance. Tom led the talk as MCD. He noted the professionalism of the crew. I commented on how training never prepares for the real thing. All felt the patients were in better shape after landing in Germany.

Robert noted that he saw me in a constant state of motion. "You were Spider-Man swinging from litter stanchion to litter stanchion . . . pushing morphine instead of shooting webs."

I observed how Jimmy and Steve could anticipate what I needed for a patient. Jeremy kept his eyes on the big picture. The towering Makah Indian guarded his territory. He was watching the interior of our makeshift hospital, looking for trouble, looking for a patient in need.

Our wounded soldiers survived. We were different now, having experienced the strain of war together. The seven of us were forever bonded by that experience. We were tested and we passed. I now knew I could count on this crew, no matter what happened.

We talked about the wounded. How impressed we were that they rarely complained. They wanted their buddies cared for first. It was unusual for someone to ask how bad his wound was. They were more concerned about their comrades. It was drastically different caring for combat wounded compared to civilians back home.

As an ER nurse or a firefighter, I tried to maintain a certain level of detachment with my patients. I put up walls. I never wanted to get to know the patient on a personal level. It was a barrier that kept me from burning out. Gallows humor helped.

It was different with these guys. They were not involved in a car accident or injured at home. They were in a war zone, defending each other, knowing that they could be wounded or killed. How many people would leave their house if they knew there was a good chance of receiving enemy fire?

They were the best from Middle America and not our nation's elite. They lived in horrible living conditions. Some wore the same uniform for months. Some hadn't showered in weeks. They lived and fought in the unforgiving, searing desert. They stank of blood, sweat, and urine. What could I do for them?

After brunch, I walked back to pack flight gear. I thought about our mission. I thought about the good food we had eaten and the room I was staying in. I felt guilty for the soft air force life I lived compared to the wounded. I had to do all I could for those soldiers and marines. They were going to get one hundred percent of my skill and time to get them home safely. They gave so much for each other, so I wanted to give something back. That's where I made a big mistake. I let my emotional walls down. The barrier I maintained at the civilian ER and as a firefighter was gone.

Another mistake: I decided that I did not want anyone to die on my watch. *Unreasonable.* At home I had seen dozens of people die, some in my own hands. It was a part of the job, and I maintained the walls. Another barrier dropped. I was going to do everything I could to keep these boys alive. We had common ground, wearing the same uniform. We fought for each other, not for a flag or national objectives. I looked at them and saw myself. Keeping them alive kept me alive. I accepted death at home, but could not accept it at war.

I continued to walk. I felt so alive. The grass was a darker, more vibrant green than I could remember. My lungs filled with the fresh air of the German countryside. Once again, I was cognizant of my own breath. Air in, chest expanded. Exhale . . . chest relaxed. This movement represented life.

Why did I feel so alive? Why did everything seem so clear? My eyes saw color that was rich and effervescent. I viewed the world differently. Perhaps only those who have been tested know what I talk about.

\* \* \*

We made our way back to England later that day. As we flew over the white cliffs of Dover, I once again thought about the bomber crews of WWII. They yearned for those cliffs that represented safety. The white cliffs served the same purpose sixty years later.

We were granted a day off, and I had a chance to send out an e-mail about our first mission. The feedback was so positive that I committed to keeping a journal of my experiences. I wanted my friends and family to understand the underside of war.

# Another Mission Downrange

## April 3, 2003 *PFC Jessica Lynch is rescued by US Forces. -CNN*

The med kits were a mess, and the supply system was fragmented at Mildenhall. It took us hours to restock our kits. We also included what we had run short of. Other returning crews started hoarding supplies too. Within a month, items like three-cc syringes and IV tubing would be in short supply.

While waiting for the next mission, we spent the time working ground support. We configured, prepped, launched, and recovered the medevac planes that flew every day. We attempted to sort the medical supply system out with little success.

## April 5–10, 2003 *US Forces secure Saddam International Airport, rename it to Baghdad International Airport. -CNN*

We traveled the lengthy, inefficient route from England to Germany, then to Sicily. In Sicily, our crew visited the ancient ruins of Agrigento. I stood on the remains of a crumbling fortress wall and looked south towards North Africa, visualizing the enemy fleet landing on the sunbaked shores and laying siege to the city. Through the centuries, mankind became experts at war. Futile.

We ate in a restaurant that was over four hundred years old. It was a massive stone structure that sweated from the walls. We attempted to stay light-hearted as the next mission loomed over our heads. Cathleen grabbed a large creamed filled cannoli and said, "Watch this."

She wrapped her lips on the end of the pastry and proceeded to suck the filling out without destroying the shell. She looked up at six men with slacked jawed faces.

"What's wrong? Isn't that a cool trick?" We stared at her in shock. Slowly it dawned on Cathleen that sucking the cannoli had a sexual connotation. She turned eight shades of red. To this day, Cathleen blushes if you say the word cannoli.

From Sicily, it was back to Kuwait for more wounded.

After landing, Rock and Bob landed right behind us. That was one of the benefits of being in the military. Wherever you went, you always ran into friends. Rock and Bob were crusty old flight engineers from the era of the C-141, which was soon to pass. With crust comes experience that will save your life during an in-flight emergency. They are the ones to fly with. Look for the crew with gray hair and crow's feet around their eyes. They will keep you alive.

We looked at each other from across the flight line, lowered our heads in mock shame, and walked towards each other. We shook hands, holding eye contact longer than most men do. We were back in the Middle East for another war. It was wearisome that we returned for more as poor lesson learners. Bob, Rock, and I had flown hundreds of hours to many of the world's hot spots: Africa, the Balkans, and Saudi Arabia in the first Gulf War. We laughed over our stupidity.

They were wearing green flight suits and makeshift shoulder holsters. The military was not spending money on guys like Bob and Rock. The C-141 aircrews would soon be gone, so no need to invest the money. Many of the front-enders like Bob and Rock did not have helmets or survival vests, yet they performed the combat entry checklist and looked outside for SAMs. I was from a modern C-17 squadron, so we were better equipped. They razzed me about my new clothes and lamented the lack of armor in the airplanes.

Unknown to me, Rock and Bob's plane hard broke. They ended up spending three days waiting for parts and enduring six air raids. (Whether a missile hits or not, one still has to put the gas mask and chem suit on.) Luckily, all returned to our base safely.

I said goodbye and promised to make a martini for them back in England. It was time to load patients, and they needed to refuel their plane.

**Rock, Bob, and I. April 2003. Camp Wolf, Kuwait International Airport.**
**Waiting for fuel and the wounded to be delivered.**

There are common themes in all of the C-141 medevac missions: long days, mission delays, and broken airplanes. But the attitude in the theater of operations had changed. Today, the ground crews and medics looked rested. There hadn't been a missile attack in over a week. Even the patients we picked up looked relaxed. On the previous mission, the patients had clutched their gas masks like newborn babies, but today, many came without chem gear.

These were not the angered patients we had last time—the ones that were distraught from ambushes, hit-and-run tactics, and the abuse of civilians. Today's casualties had colorful, animated stories of firefights and taking prisoners. They were willing to explain to us, in minute detail, the events of the battles and how they were wounded.

Joe, a young marine, was shooting at an Iraqi to his right when two more started shooting to his left. He engaged the left side while the first Iraqi outflanked him and shot him in the back. The bullet went though the gap below the shoulder of his body armor. It passed though his chest, ricocheted off the front armor plate, and skimmed out the left side of his body armor. As Joe was telling his story, he was making direct eye contact with me, but I could tell he wasn't seeing me. He was reliving every moment of the battle. His hands were in motion describing the details, and his words were fraught with emotion, but his eyes told most of the story.

A soldier with shrapnel wounds spoke of taking prisoners. He believed the war would be over if they didn't have to stop to take prisoners. "The volume of prisoners is slowing us down. We'd advance a lot faster if we could figure out a faster way of getting Iraqi POWs off the field."

This soldier also talked about the effect Iraqi treatment of American POWs was having on the ground troops. Thanks in part to the rumors about how PFC Lynch was treated in her captivity, this GI's squad had made a pact that they would fix bayonets before they allowed themselves to be captured. Astonished, I asked, "Are you aware of any of our forces having to fix bayonets?"

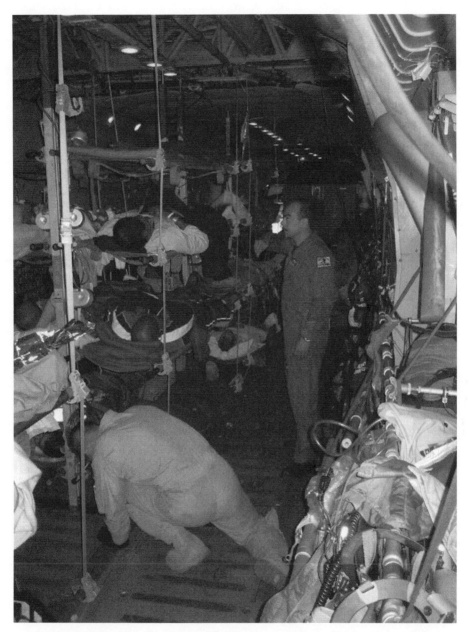

After loading checklist. Securing patients in the stanchions. Giving patient briefings
on emergency procedures for ditching and oxygen masks. Jeremy is kneeling
to lock the stanchion in place so the litters will not sway in flight.

He said, "No. American airstrikes don't allow the Iraqis that close."

The man who made the most significant impression was a tank commander with a neck wound. This first sergeant was leading when a rocket-propelled grenade glanced off the armor of his M-1 tank. The shrapnel struck him in the neck. This sergeant was not the typical young, twenty-ish GI in for a four-year stint. He was a professional soldier and a veteran of the first Gulf War. He had a genuine sense of duty and dedication that is usually seen only in career non-commissioned officers (NCOs). He was not happy about being evaced out of the war zone. He explained, "I need to get back to my boys and take care of business." This man was a classic example of the backbone of our military.

It was hard not to think about the severely wounded. The injuries were devastating and permanent. They would never return to the life they used to know. Life was forever changed.

In reflecting on my patients, I realized that this flight was just the beginning of their journeys home. Some would return to duty, some would never fully recover. All would carry the memories of the war. I could not help but think about the men that went home to their wives and children mentally and physically different. I thought about the nineteen-year-old who had lost most of his feet. What would the future hold for him? And what of the critically injured who had a long future of VA hospitals followed by VA disability? How would they cope? How would they adjust?

I felt obligated to stay out there and take care of the wounded. The tank commander told me he could not do my job. He didn't enjoy being sequestered on our flying hospital and looking at the aftermath of war. He didn't understand how I dealt with taking care of the consequences. But my job was easy compared to leading tanks into battle.

\*\*\*

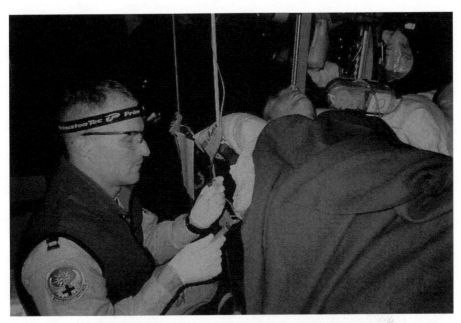

**Pushing IV morphine to subdue the pain of a combat wound.**
**In-flight care on a C-141 medevac transport. April 2003.**

When we landed in Spain, ground operations were running smoothly and efficiently. The AEOT and MASF were in place to support Fleet Hospital 8. We were greeted at the aircraft by members of our home squadron at McChord. They requested that we deplane and said that they would take care of the off-load. The wounded, our equipment, the filthy neglected jet, were all handled by the ground support. We shuffled to debriefing, with BBQ and beer waiting. That's how the air force fights a war.

The following day I spent exploring the base and relaxing. As I walked back towards the sea huts, I saw the wounded tank commander walking towards me. He was still in his tanker coveralls and had no hat on. I said hello and reached out to shake his hand. It was strong, callused, and cracked dry from the desert heat. I was not in uniform, and the first sergeant searched a minute in order to recognize that I was one of the medevac nurses.

He immediately apologized for not having a hat on. "All I have is my coveralls and my ID card. Everything else is back in Iraq, sir." This sergeant was a towering, powerful man. My first thought was that I hoped I never pissed that guy off. I asked him how his wound was.

"No problem, sir," he responded as I look at the white bandage covering his tan neck. "I'm working on getting back to my unit. I finally convinced the docs that I'm fit for duty." Fit for duty? If that shrapnel had gone just a little further into his neck, his jugular vein and carotid artery would have been severed. He came very close to being killed. All this guy wanted was to get back to his men. I was thinking he should spend some time off in Spain and enjoy the second chance he was granted.

We talked about the war, and I asked him if he thought it is worth it. The sergeant fixed his eyes with mine and said, "You know, a reporter asked me the same question right after one of my boys got killed. No, it's not worth it. Nothing is worth one of my boys losing his life. They drive their cars at our tanks with women and children in them. My boys hesitate at shooting them. I push them. They have to shoot. You don't know if that car is loaded with explosives or if it just has women and children in it. There is no time for hesitation. That's why I have to get back to them. It's not worth them losing their lives."

I agreed. "I'm having a hard time making sense of it all myself. All I get to see is the wounded. How do you tell someone that just lost his leg that it's worth it?"

The sergeant now looked past me. His eyes narrowed like Clint Eastwood. I saw the wrinkles by his eyes sharpen as he focused on another soldier walking towards us from a distance. For the first time, he raised his voice. "You see that piece of shit walking towards us? I saw him at battalion aid limping. Do you see him limping now?" He was walking normal. "That piece of shit is trying to get out of his duty. I have my guys fighting and dying and this guy is scamming. I wish he was in my unit. I'd get on his ass and get him back out there." The soldier walked by smiling, within earshot of us. We were both quiet. The two soldiers locked eyes. The sergeant stared into his soul. His face said, "I know you are a fake, how can you stand yourself?" The soldier's eyes dropped to the ground, and he continued on without the smile. He knew that the sergeant knew. I thought for sure the sergeant was going grab the soldier with one hand and crush his windpipe. It was not his troop, not his problem. He was too professional to lash out at the sad sack.

The encounter with the slacking soldier ruined our conversation. We said our goodbyes and good lucks. The entire time we talked, he called me sir and gave the proper respect NCOs give an officer. I should have been calling him sir.

I continued my walk and thought about the caliber of this tank commander. Where did the military find such men? Not from Harvard or Yale. This was an average American likely raised in the rural Midwest, working a farm or construction.

# April 10, 2003

The crew departed Spain and returned home to England. Back again to the routine of restocking medical kits and working ground support. Some of the equipment shortages were covered by the hospital at Lakenheath, a fifteen-minute drive from base. A bean counter realized we had no way to pay for the materials and cut us off. We then ordered stores though a warehouse in Germany. This was part of the NATO stockpile, a relic of the Cold War. Before, shortages were covered the same day, but now it took a week to restock. The patients were never affected by the supply shortages. Somehow we always managed to find what was needed to complete the mission. It was the creativity of the aircrews and ground support that kept the missions moving, not military logistics.

Another example of this was the shortage of litters at Camp Wolf, Kuwait. The medics asked to bring more litters. I asked our chief nurse if she could arrange for empty litters to be flown down to Kuwait. She told me, "That's not an air force problem. Supply is handled by the army. They need to work that out." I didn't argue with her as I counted our growing collection of empty litters. I was in no position to mediate a conversation between the army and air force.

The simple solution was for medical crews to sneak litters onto the plane after it was loaded with cargo downrange. After the pallets were in place, we would lash bundles of litters on top of the load. It was unregulated cargo, but the medics would now have their litters. We did this until the end of June, when the army and air force finally worked out the supply problems.

Baghdad airport was secured. Rumors were flying about how quickly the war would end, which also meant how quickly we would go home. There was talk of some of the squadron going home as soon as Iraq was free. Another rumor started that we would be flying evac missions into Baghdad. We were briefed before we left the States that this was a possibility. I really didn't think the air force would risk such an easy, unarmed target. I could picture a medical transport loaded with wounded on board being shot down over Baghdad.

## April 16, 2003 *Marines attempting to secure a government building are assaulted by townspeople with rocks and fists. –CNN*

It took a few days to get reassigned to another mission. Not because there was a lack of wounded, and not because the war looked like it would be over soon. The inefficiency of our evac system and the poor reliability of the C-141 kept us on the ground.

We eventually made it back to Sicily and sat on BRAVO alert waiting for another mission. I continued to write while we waited for the phone to ring.

On return flights, I tried to update my journal and flight log. So much was happening that gaps existed in my records. Sleep deprivation was a part of it. Even at that early stage of the war, we were having maintenance and supply problems.

I noted that, as of April 8, we had managed one on-time takeoff out of Sigonella. The aircraft continued to be plagued by the filter bypass light. This caution light told us that we had fuel contamination. We were not sure what was happening, and it was suspected that our fuel was being tampered with downrange. The bypass light came on during high-power settings, such as takeoff, or climbing to altitude. Takeoffs were aborted because of this. The pilots had to slam on the brakes to keep us from rolling off the end of the runway during these rejected flight attempts.

On one leg from England to Germany, it took twelve hours to get between the two places. This was normally an hour-and-a-half flight. We had a rejected takeoff and two air aborts. Those delays coupled with our extended flight path made it difficult to complete a single mission. In spite of this, morale was still high, and we were motivated to fly. The troops we took care of were also motivated.

We had an added role for our air evac missions: returning healed casualties to their field units. What caught my eye a few days prior to this trip was a sergeant who walked onto our plane with a cast on his left arm.

Estrada was a platoon sergeant for a transportation company moving supplies into Iraq. He was in a convoy of about seventy vehicles when they came under an RPG (rocket-propelled grenade) ambush. He shared with me the events that caused his wounds: "The RPGs started hitting wildly around the convoy. The fire was not accurate at all. I immediately returned fire with the SAW [squad automatic weapon, a light machine gun]. Honestly I had no idea what I was shooting at. All I could see was sand. There was lots of outgoing fire. It was not controlled at first, but then the security force with us started coordinating our response. An RPG exploded on the front bumper of my vehicle. Shrapnel from the grenade passed through my left hand and dislodged two of my knuckles. That was it for me. Soon after, the security detail took care of those that ambushed us."

Sgt. Estrada was wounded on April 7 and was already returning to duty on April 15. In those eight days, he said he received the best care of his life. The medical personnel all down the line were professional and helpful every step of the way. "They gave me new clothes, good food, a shower, and the Purple Heart medal. Anything I needed was provided at the army hospital."

Like many of my patients, I asked the sergeant how he felt about the Purple Heart. Movies portray the medal as an honorable thing—a badge of courage. I've always wondered if the wounded see the medal the same way. Sgt. Estrada said that getting hurt was not the way to earn a medal. However, he did tell me, "I understand that by having the Purple Heart, it will open some doors for scholarships and education benefits for my children. If somehow their lives are improved by this, maybe getting wounded will be worth it." Sgt. Estrada also realized how lucky he was not to lose his hand. The doctors told him he should make a full recovery after some follow-up surgery.

The platoon sergeant was scheduled to fly stateside for that very surgery, but he knew if he left Europe he would never get back to his unit. He explained, "My lieutenant is only twenty-two years old and has only been in our unit five months. She has a lot of potential but has not developed her field sense yet. Most of my troops are nineteen and twenty years old. I'm like a father to them." I could relate. We were both thirty-four.

This veteran of sixteen years felt he had an obligation to return to his unit even though he had been wounded and ordered home. The Sgt. had a family in the US and knew they were safe. His military family in Iraq needed him more. Sgt. Estrada requested to be returned to duty and was told instead that he was going home. He did not give up. He continued to ask up the chain of command until he finally met a colonel at Landstuhl Army Medical Center. The colonel said he would sign his return to duty, but only if he called his mother first. Sgt. Estrada told me with a big smile that he pleaded with his mother, "I need to get back to my boys. . . . Please don't ask me home." With that, he was released for duty.

I asked the sergeant about the cast on his left arm. "How will you handle the SAW now?"

Sgt. Estrada educated me on his role in the platoon. "They will give me a Beretta when I get back. I can still shoot with my right hand. I'm not really supposed to fight. My job will be to guide and direct the platoon and help my new LT (military slang for lieutenant) as much as possible." He was another example of the dedication and sense of duty our non-commissioned officers have for the soldiers under their watchful eye.

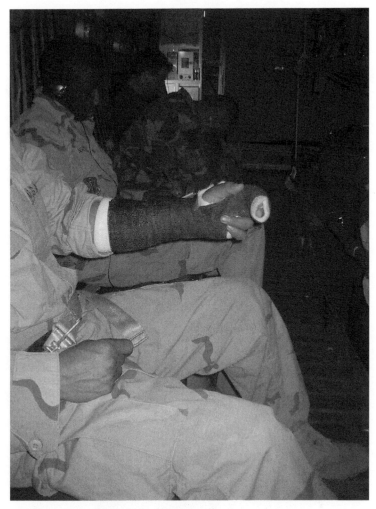

**Wounded troop, returning to combat.**

We swapped crews in Sicily and went into crew rest. The plane continued on to Kuwait with Sgt. Estrada. I never saw him again, but he continues to inspire me.

# A Med-Evac Mission on Easter Day

## April 20, 2003

Over Easter weekend we were alerted for thirty-five casualties. The mission was textbook perfect. No dramas, no medical emergencies, no Scud attacks, and no maintenance delays. We were on time and on-target. The flight back to Germany emphasized the simple needs of humanity.

I used to be a civilian and worked in an emergency room in Tacoma. Every once in a while, a patient would make an impression on me that I would never forget. Sometimes that impression would remind me of the frailty of humanity. Sometimes the memory would give me nightmares.

Now I had been recalled to active duty and was flying wounded out of the Middle East. Every one of my patients was making an impression on me. Each one had a story to tell, and I tried to listen. This was a different kind of nursing. I was finding that my ears healed just as much as my hands. For the solider, the eight- to ten-hour flight out of the war zone was their chance to defuse and sort their thoughts. It was the first time they were safe and did not have to worry about incoming fire. It was their first time they could let their guards down and relax.

Some came onto the plane with the thousand-yard stare. Some came on with eyes darting about, assessing the new environment, maybe looking for an ambush or a booby trap. Some walked with a nervous jitter, some walked on like zombies. Some had eyes glazed over from a morphine-induced stupor.

Once we were at cruising altitude, you could feel the tension drop within the aircraft. The medics and nurses worked and listened. The hard faces began to smile, and the soldiers changed. There was a metamorphosis from combat veteran back to the nineteen-year-old kid just out of high school. There was a common pattern to the conversation. We talked about the combat action and how they were wounded. As the flight hours passed, the talk changed to home: men who wanted to see their girlfriends or wives, men who want to hold their children again, marines that savored the thought of an ice-cold beer, soldiers that wanted to see the latest issue of *Playboy* magazine.

I thought I was doing a decent job at nursing when my medical crew discovered a cure-all on our Easter Day mission. We had collected money at our staging base and bought frozen pizzas and cookie dough. Halfway through the flight, we started cooking the pizzas. I walked from patient to patient and asked them if they would like a pizza. There were looks of disbelief. These boys had seen nothing but MREs for over three months. The smell of pizza started to drift from our aircraft ovens (we had five small convection ovens on the plane). Looks of anticipation developed.

Our crew passed out the pizza to the faces of eager boys. They did not look like combat veterans anymore. Most of them had the gleeful looks of young children at an Easter egg hunt. We just gave them a little taste of home and America. The pizza worked better than any drug I could administer. They joked and laughed with each other. For a while, they forgot about their wounds.

I didn't mention the cookie dough. After the pizza, we brought out the fresh-baked cookies (which took a little skill in a pressurized cabin). The cookies were hot and dripping chocolate. The med crew weaved between the seats and litter stanchions and let the boys grab the gooey cookies. You should have seen the looks on their faces. I imagine it was the same look I gave my mom when she made cookies.

It was on this Easter Day mission that I realized that there was more to healing the wounds of war than pushing drugs and dressing injuries.

I have to give credit where credit is due. Major Marlin, at the crew management cell in Sicily, came up with the idea of buying pizza for the troops. I was in charge of the mission and did not think we had time to cook pizza and cookies. I wanted to continue to serve the MREs. She convinced me to take the pizzas, and I'm glad she did. Thank you Major Marlin. I was wrong, and you were right.

I snapped a photo of some of the marines we brought home on Easter. I do my best to protect the identities of these guys. I wanted to capture their faces, though you still don't know their names or injuries. This was what those boys looked like when they first got on the plane, before we had a chance to work with them. Sometimes the looks they would give at first scared me. I wish I had a photo of these marines at the end of the mission. A completely different, relaxed look.

We passed patients to Fleet Hospital 8, signed in gear and weapons, and looked forward to crew rest in Spain. I checked for old-fashioned mail. Moving to a different country every third or fourth day, the mail could not catch up.

I was not too worried about mail. E-mail had replaced written letters. I remembered the first Gulf War, how I looked forward to and lived for mail call. A week without mail was depressing. The information age brought my friends and family to me instantly. During Iraqi Freedom, I rarely received mail. Most everyone I knew used e-mail.

**Combat marines with captured Iraqi battle flag. These marines got this flag at Baghdad University. They did not find it. They fought for it. When they first got to the university, the flag was flying proudly by Iraqi regulars. It is clear who won the battle.**

The letters in the first Gulf War were never more than five days old. For Iraqi Freedom, the mail consistently took three to four weeks to catch up.

I was now typing war stories, e-mailed on a regular basis. I found that writing helped pass the time in BRAVO alert. Writing caused me to reflect on the previous mission. There was a side effect to my penned work: it broke down any remaining barriers that I may have had. The writing exposed my feelings instead of suppressing them within. Crewing evac missions was becoming emotional.

I had a difficult night of sleep. I dreamt of wounded. I woke up tired and wrote another e-mail home. I didn't notice, but my stories were changing as the war started to affect me. I wrote about the casualty with the open wound.

## An Open Wound, April 23, 2003

The best way to describe his injuries was to say that chunks of his body were missing. He was in a lot of pain. He smelled, was dirty, and had bandages that were leaking blood and serous fluid. The field hospital didn't have time to clean him up since he was a priority patient to evacuate.

I had noticed that the most seriously injured were the youngest. The older, experienced soldiers did a better job of staying alive and avoiding the flying metal. This soldier seemed like a young boy. We talked for a bit as I assessed him. I medicated him for his pain. It was the first of many infusions.

The morphine was not working, but it was the strongest stuff I had. I had to play a juggling act to keep my patient comfortable. He was bedridden and unable to move what was left of his extremities. I was constantly moving pillows, adjusting his position, and giving morphine— lots of morphine. I ended up giving him more morphine than I had to all of the other patients on the aircraft combined, and still he was not comfortable.

At some point during these adjustments, I accidentally dislodged a Hemovac suction unit from one of his infected wounds. Foul smelling, reddish-yellow fluid drained from the tube and dripped off the litter. I started looking at his bandages to find the other end of the tubing. I opened one bandage and found sand fleas where his toes use to be. I tried my best to keep a straight face, but the sight of the fleas in his wound nauseated me. Steve, one of my levelheaded medics, found the tubing and reset the suction, then cleaned up the mess I made. Steve maintained a cool composure, though I still felt disturbed and pale.

We finally got the soldier comfortable. Because we moved him so much, I decided to reassess his extremities. The circulation was poor at the end of his legs, and what was left of his feet was swollen. I knew there were parts of his leg and thigh missing from reading his medical record, but I couldn't tell from the thick bandages. The wounds were left open to allow them to drain. The dressings were wet and covered in a light layer of sand.

I asked the soldier to wiggle the toes he had. We made direct eye contact. How I acted then was very important to him. On one side his toes moved fine; on the other side there was no movement. What was left on that side was cold and hard to touch. He looked at me and our eyes are locked. His eyes said, "Tell me I'm going to be okay. Tell me that I'm going to be fine, tell me I'm going to be whole again. . . . " Those were some of the longest seconds of my life, because I knew he was counting on what I said to him.

I bent down below the litter to break eye contact. I acted like I was adjusting some of the medical equipment attached to him. My mind was racing. I had always been honest with my patients. Should I lie or tell him the truth? The seconds moved so slowly as I fought my internal battle on what was right. I stood straight up, and there were his eyes. I was at the end of the litter, and with the noise of the plane there was no way he could hear me speak. We were now communicating solely with our eyes and facial expressions. The look on his face . . . the look . . . I felt like what I did next would determine his future.

I was sure less than two seconds had passed before I gave him a big smile and a thumb's up. Those two seconds felt like an hour. He broke into a big smile of relief, and I felt broken for lying to him. He motioned to me and I walked to the head of the litter. I leaned in so he could yell into my ear over the jet noise. "Why do my feet feel so cold?" he asked.

I yelled back, "There's a lot of swelling in your feet and the blood circulation is not so good because of the swelling. It is way too early in the game to tell how well you are going to heal. The swelling is going to affect your senses and ability to move." These were all true statements. I felt reassured with my answer. It was too early to say how this soldier would recover. But I still felt bad about lying.

As the flight continued, we burned off fuel, the plane's weight decreased, and we could climb higher. The higher the plane was, the more efficiently it flew; the higher we flew, the greater the internal cabin altitude.

Jimmy, another one of our hard-working medics, reported that my patient's oxygen level was dropping. I checked the altimeter on my watch and saw that our cabin altitude was now at six thousand feet. We started out at a two thousand-foot cabin altitude. This created a viscous circle for my patient. I had given him a lot of morphine, which caused him to breathe shallow breaths, and the six thousand-foot cabin altitude had caused his breathing rate to increase. The increased breathing rate was making his body work harder, which then burned the morphine faster. The rapid, shallow breathing dropped his blood-oxygen level. Jimmy placed oxygen on my patient to raise his oxygen level, but this also made him more alert. He was more aware of what was going on and wanted more morphine. I couldn't win.

I did a quick mental calculation in my head:
the cabin altitude, the amount of flight time
left, and the amount of morphine I could safely
give him. It was a juggling act. I spent the
remainder of the flight close to his side. I
never got him completely pain free, but I strove
for a medium between an adequate oxygen level
and manageable pain. It reminded me very much
of caring for cancer patients.

I was spent. I looked at my patient and saw that
he was in pain again. I gave him a final dose
of morphine so he could tolerate the ambulance
ride to the hospital. I went to the bar to get
a dose of gin so I could sleep.

Captain Ed 'RIV' Hrivnak,

Instructor Flight Nurse

491 Expeditionary Aeromedical Evacuation
Squadron

I sent the e-mail, closed out the computer, and dressed to run hoping that a five-mile jog would clear my brain.

\*\*\*

The drinking after a mission helped me sleep. We had been flying for a month. The long days were creeping up on my well being. Every third day we were sleeping in another time zone, often flying at night and sleeping during the day. The crew's circadian rhythm was not rhythmic. I rarely felt completely rested. I had a few drinks at night and a couple cups of coffee during the day. A creature comfort from Washington State, I traveled with a French press and Starbucks espresso beans. The coffee was thick black syrup brewed to keep the dead moving. It was a cycle of uppers (caffeine) and downers (alcohol) to get through the mission.

When not flying at night, we rotated to day shift to load and unload the wounded, pack medical kits, or work hospital rounds. It didn't occur to anyone that months of moving hundreds of wounded might have an effect on our spirit. Months after I was home, I figured it out.

After e-mails and breakfast, my crew made rounds at the hospital. That day we were preparing a load from Fleet Hospital 8 to fly back to the States. Preparation consisted of reviewing the patient charts to ensure the casualties were stable enough to fly to the US. We checked that the patient had enough medications for flight and that dressing and IVs were taken care of. We coordinated with GPMRC (global patient management regulation center . . . *always have to have an acronym in the military*). GPMRC was at Scott AFB, Illinois. Patients couldn't fly until they had been regulated through GPMRC. It was a challenge working with an agency halfway around the world. Time and distance created confusion. The information they had was dated compared to the actual patient in front of me.

The question was asked, "Is that patient regulated?" The process dehumanized them. We were regulating human cargo to load onto the cavernous plane. The living freight fed the jet so it could continue on the next leg of its never-ending journey in this never-ending war.

I nonchalantly referred to our patients as the load for the day. This day was 18-35 + 2: eighteen litters, thirty-five ambulatory, and two attendants. Forget that each casualty was a human with a personality and a story to tell. What happened to them in Iraq? Each human package had a family at home, worried and waiting for them—and waiting for us to load the commodities.

I entered the vestibule of the fleet hospital. My feet floated on the inflatable hallways that connected the tent wards together. Even in Spain, sand was everywhere. Military tent cities always had sand. Heavy spring rains had flooded parts of the hospital. My feet traversed from sand, to water, to the inflate-o-tubes, and then through mud.

I was searching the wards to find a patient and instead got lost in the maze of Fleet Hospital 8. I turned and walked into my boy who was missing part of his feet, toes, and legs. We recognized each other. There was no longer the noise of the jet to keep us from talking, but we still communicated with our eyes. He was excited and happy as I masked my shame for withholding the truth. The young soldier pulled the blanket away so I could see his feet.

"Look at my feet Cap'n." I looked down. The swelling had reduced, and some color had returned to his lower legs. I looked closer at his toes and saw that the ones he had left were wiggling at me. "I can move my toes Cap'n."

I wanted to break down and cry. A wave of suppressed emotion overcame me, and I fought to keep it inside. So much for dehumanizing the load for the day, I thought to myself. The feelings bubbled out of my stomach and reached up to my throat as bile. That's where I stopped them and pushed it back down. I was this boy's nurse. He counted on me to be strong. He relied on me to be there for him. I wouldn't break down in front of him. I buried my feelings, reached over, and shook hands. He thanked me and I said, "Never give up hope." I quickly left the ward, looking for an exit, needing fresh air. The smells of hospital and rubber walls were bringing the bile back up. The inflatable halls were collapsing on me.

I found the outside, rushed across a field of water and mud, and hid behind the open door of a Conex box. I leaned against the box and let the feelings out, hiding so no one could see. I cried, heaved, and vomited. The weight of duty was crushing me. I fought to catch my breath. The boy had a chance, but he would never be the same. I would never be the same. I went back in the hospital, finished rounds, and got the load right. I fed the plane with bodies and then fed my body a martini to deaden the pain.

# Life in Crew Rest

## April 30, 2003

In crew rest, I tried to track down Jennifer. Her e-mails were infrequent and just a few sentences long. Phone calls were out of the question, changing continents weekly. I received a message from a transiting C-130 crew that she had moved to the Afghan theater of operations.

In March, there was little free time. The war had slowed down, our workdays had improved, and we had more downtime. When aircrews had time off, mischief occurred. Waywardness included skinny-dipping in the ocean, M*A*S*H parties, and exploring the unknown in Europe. Whatever the case, this time to blow off steam always included drinking.

It had been a long-standing tradition for aircrews to drink after a mission—to toast a safe return and honor those who didn't make it back. Sometimes aircrews needed a drink to steady their hands after a long, dangerous mission. This tradition dates back to World War I, when Captain Eddie Rickenbacker was downing German planes on the western front. The ritual expanded to English pubs during World War II, when 8th Air Force bomber crews returned from missions over Europe. F-105

Thud pilots would enjoy a drink in Thailand after fighting over Vietnam.

In the modern air force, our missions were long duty days— often twenty-six hours. Exhaustion and a few drinks caused flyers to pass out. This had initiated a new game.

The first person to drop won having their finger and toe nails painted with bright red polish. I was the original person to be initiated into this ritual. Dragged awake for a mission, I realized too late that my nails were a brilliant ruby red. I flew the entire evac route with painted fingers and toes. My worst fear was that we would be shot down and I would become the boyfriend of an Iraqi prison guard. Nail polish remover was a challenge to find. Someone kept buying all the bottles of polish remover at the BX (on base store), making it difficult to clean the colorful nails.

I left my buddies Rock and Bob down in the Middle East. Their plane broke, and they spent three days avoiding Scud alerts before returning to Europe. When they landed in England, I had a drink waiting for them. Those guys were exhausted. Most of their crew hadn't made it for the post-mission drink. They had gone straight to bed. But Rock and Bob were true aircrew. They were the guys you would have found in the upper ball turret of a wounded B-17 bomber over Berlin. They were committed flyers and would not think of breaking tradition.

I made my infamous martini, which was making its rounds among the C-141 aircrews. After two drinks, Rock was out cold. I was proud to continue this long-standing air force custom.

So that someone can carry the tradition on for the next generation of aircrews, I share my secret recipe:

Take a Lewis bag filled with ice and pound the ice until it is in fine ice chips. Dump the ice into a stainless steel shaker.
Add vodka or gin that has been stored in a freezer.
Fill shaker 7/8 full.
Then add two drops of English bitters and one slice of lime.
Shake for forty-five seconds.
Pour in a martini glass that contains two spiced Sicilian olives.

Little shavings of ice will float on top of the drink.

This drink hides pain well.

We drank until we ran out of booze or until someone passed out. Yeah, we were exhausted. But we almost always drank after a mission. One problem we had with our martinis is that we could not find any real martini glasses. The best I could find were margarita glasses. We'd get drunk pretty easily with the margarita martini glasses. A normal martini glass holds four ounces of liquid. I measured our margarita glasses to find they held ten ounces of vodka. No wonder we were drunk after just one of them.

Where the crew slept was in constant flux. One day it was a hotel in Germany, the next week you could be sleeping on a cot in a hangar. This was a unique reverse lodging for our crew. It seemed like the closer we got to the war, the better our accommodations were. The worst place we slept was an open tent by the flight line at Wright-Patterson AFB, Ohio. But later, when we stayed in Kuwait, we were in a five-star hotel. The spoiled aircrew that had gotten used to the plush accommodations could not understand why we weren't treated as royalty everywhere we went. We were *Air Force Aircrew*, perhaps the most spoiled of all the military. One of the shelters that did not meet standards but did provide for team building was the sea huts.

In Spain there was a shortage of housing for the medical crews. The navy Seabees built us wooden shelters to live in. Typical of Seabees, they named our shelters "sea huts."

The sea huts were similar to Camp Heritage when I was a teenage Boy Scout. I mentally pretended I was in the scouts again. Twelve to fourteen people lived in a hut at any given time. The quarters were tight, and there was much complaining. No minibar, high tea, or remote-controlled TVs.

The navy fleet hospital was camped next to us in mildewed army canvas tents. That did not lessen the complaints. You really got to know the people you bunked with.

Major Tom was someone I had come to know very well. We had shared the same room, hut, or tent since the start of this war. At this point, we were a boring married couple with our daily routine.

I made the coffee while he took a shower. He loaded the martini glasses with olives while I shook the vodka and bitters.

Like anyone that had lived together in close quarters, there were habits that annoyed me about Tom. Actually, there was only one thing that irritated me about Tom: his loud, obnoxious snoring. I lost a lot of quality sleep because of Tom's snoring. It had no rhythm or cadence. The level of noise rose and fell inconsistently. I tried earplugs. He tried nose strips. Nothing rid my nights of the noise.

One night the snoring stopped. Tom was having a moment of apnea. I prayed to myself, *please let him die!* Alas, the snoring started up again, but louder—and this time with a vengeance. I thought about where my survival knife was.

Then we moved into the sea huts. Twelve men in a wooden box. Our first night in the huts, I was punished for wishing Tom's death; ten of the twelve men in the hut snored. We also had a rainstorm and high winds that night.

I had just settled into the top bunk, which put me within arms reach of the rafters. The wind blew against the hut. I could hear the wood creak and bend. The rain pelted against the aluminum roof, generating a roar against the metal. Then the snoring kicked in.

Ten grown men were snoring at different rates and rhythms. There was no chorus or harmony. The wood of the hut continued to twist and contort in the wind. The snoring crashed like waves against a boat. A bead of water formed on the rafter above my head. I felt like a seaman on an ancient Spanish galleon. The volume of snoring gave a sensation of movement. I thought I might get seasick in the sea hut. Sleep eluded me that night.

The next morning, I apologized to Major Tom for wishing him dead. His snoring, compared to that of the ten men, was like a mother lulling a child to sleep. I had learned my lesson: don't complain about what you have, because it *can* get worse.

We ended up living in the sea huts for twelve days before our next mission. At the end of those twelve days, every one of us had a dry, hacking cough. We had many theories about the cough. The flight surgeon thought it was a virus and said not to worry about it. Some said there was mold in the huts. A navy Seabee thought the treated wood in the hut leached arsenic when it got wet. Camp story? Two weeks later and I was still coughing.

# "Mission Accomplished"

May 1, 2003 *My fellow Americans, major combat operations in Iraq have ended. In the battle of Iraq, the United States and our allies have prevailed.–George W. Bush*

A crowd of airmen stood around a TV and watched the commander in chief land on an aircraft carrier and give the infamous speech in front of a large banner announcing, "Mission Accomplished." The President's speech made us feel our job was nearly done. I believed our President and was proud of what we had accomplished. I really thought the war was almost over.

*Sucker.*

We had not flown in ten days. We were on the hook, but there were no planes. I had complained to CMC and the chief nurse that we had too many crews. I did not like sitting around. I didn't like ground support. I wanted to fly, but the missions had dried up. I insisted we needed to send some people home.

Every morning we would check in and then get released for the day, taking day trips to explore Spain. The crew watched a bull fight and visited Gibraltar.

We learned intimate details about each other.

Robert was chronically late for our day trips. He enjoyed long showers and wearing offensive cologne, earning him the name "Foo Foo." Robert didn't drink, but I cut him slack (I liked having drinking partners) because he was our international designated driver.

Jimmy was gifted at wooing foreign women by making origami creatures out of dollar bills.

I enjoyed making martinis and was a slob at keeping my room. My travel bags exploded after a mission, and Jeremy hated me for it. The crew called me "Spider-Man" or "RIV," my air force nickname.

Jeremy would stay out late patrolling for women while drinking at bars. He was given the moniker "Night Stalker." He was also "Loo boy" from continued problems with international bathrooms.

Steve was the rock of our crew, unwavering. He caused no incidents, though he witnessed plenty.

Tom kept us all together as a family and medevac crew. We were a small continent-hopping military unit with a specific mission: preserve life. Tom was in command and affectionately named "Major Tom."

Our crew enjoyed the days off together. We had become exceptionally close. Cathleen was so comfortable that she asked Robert to put sunburn lotion on her back after enjoying the beach too long. Without hesitation, Cathleen lifted her shirt over her head to expose her back. She was that relaxed with us. Her skin was lobster red. But none of us noticed. She wasn't wearing a bra, and we were trying not to stare. I couldn't help but observe how firm her stomach was. We were so used to seeing Cathleen in uniform that it hadn't occurred to us what she looked like underneath.

After she left the hut, I mentioned that maybe one of the guys should tell her not to do that again. We were men who thought like boys. And we were boys who had not seen a naked woman in months. Nothing was said. We assumed we were going home soon.

We were staffed to handle three missions a day. The war had fizzled. I started thinking about Washington State. Many of us felt we would be home in thirty days. Orders came down for half the squadron to rotate home. Unfortunately, they split our crew. Jeremy, Tom, and I stuck together, but the rest of our talented crew was either sent home or to new assignments.

Our last night as a group, we rented a room at the navy lodge and reminisced about our time together. We were family very different from my own.

I have a beautiful wife Jennifer, and a mildly competitive twin brother, Eric. The three of us, all reservists, were all recalled to active duty. My wife was in Pakistan, and my brother was flying missions all over the world. I had not seen either of them since the end of February. Back in the States were my mom, brothers, sisters, in-laws, and nephews. They were family, but right then their presence seemed very distant, as though from another lifetime.

My medevac crew was family while overseas. There were seven of us—brothers and sisters all. None of us really knew each other before the war. We came from different professions, cultures, and different parts of the US. Some of us had flown together prior to war, but we did not *know* each other. We had been living together under close contact and stressful conditions.

The forced environment had, in some respects, brought us closer than our biological families. It was a union from conflict. Most civilians wouldn't understand the intensity and strength of our relationship. A fire department may have a sense of family. A night shift crew at an emergency department may taste the same closeness. But it's not the same. Back home, the medics and nurses go home to their families. They can take vacations. We got days off, but because of alert schedules, we took our days off together. Our time was consumed in each other's company. I spent more time with my crew on a daily basis than I did with my own wife at home.

I would be performing a procedure on a patient, and the medics could anticipate the needed equipment. After flying awhile, we didn't need to speak to each other; we functioned as one. Eye contact, hand signals, body language, and the environment around us had become our means of communication. Even if we could have gotten time away from each other, we wouldn't have.

What happened in each of our lives became shared experience. When Robert's son was injured at home, it was important to all of us that his child was okay. When one of us was sick, we were all there for support. If someone was short on money, the crew would cover them without an expectation of reimbursement. Getting drinks at a bar was never an issue—at times we fought over who was going to buy the next round. When we had disagreements with each other, we fought about it, resolved it, and moved on. There was no backstabbing among my crew.

I have flown with hundreds of crews over the last sixteen years. Somehow that air evac crew had the right mix of personality and experience to create a well-blended team. I will forever cherish the experience of serving with those nurses and medics. It was a privilege to serve with Tom, Cathleen, Robert, Steve, Jimmy, and Jeremy. They will always be my friends.

**The best medical evacuation crew I ever flew with. From left top to right bottom: SSgt. Jimmy Natio, TSgt. Robert Berareas, TSgt. Steve Nueves, Major Tom Hansen, Lt. Cathleen Likens, Capt. Ed Hrivnak, SSgt. Jeremy Parker.**

# Battle Buddies and
# a Mission Stateside

## Early May 2003

With our days on the ground in Spain, we continued to labor over the ground ops of medical evacuation. We worked with Fleet Hospital 8 and prepped patients for flights, loading them on a C-141 jet going to the United States. Our own aeromedical evacuation operations team (AEOT) from the McChord reserves served as the liaison for operations out of Spain.

Evac crews flying through the different staging bases took turns working with the AEOT. We did our best to make the transition from the hospital to the airplane as smooth as possible for the patients.

Often we experienced military SNAFUs. Refueling would be delayed, the plane would have a maintenance problem, or any number of things could go wrong with launching the mission. It could be as simple as a broken seal on a toilet. Because of that, the patients sometimes waited for hours on the flight line to be loaded.

Those marines and soldiers were very good at waiting. They learned it at basic training. Hurry up and wait. They saw that we were doing our best and didn't complain. One soldier, trying his best to be patient, went too long between morphine shots. He tried to gut it out. He did not want to slow the loading of the airplane. We loaded him on the bottom rack, and he immediately grabbed onto the litter above him. I looked down and saw his knuckles turn white, as he had a death grip on the litter crossbeam. Tears poured down his face, but he did not make a sound. I grabbed the primary flight nurse and told him to give the kid some of the good stuff. The nurse said he would get the morphine when we were done loading the rest of the litter patients.

I can't blame the nurse. It was his first real casualty mission in the war. It is easy to lose sight of one patient and get caught up in what was going around you. It was sometimes easy to forget that the needs of the patient should always come first. The needs of the patient should dictate how a mission was managed.

I shouted to the nurse to toss me a syringe of morphine and that I would take care of him. When I returned to the GI, a battle buddy was holding his hand and talking softly. Their hands were locked like they were ready to arm wrestle. I quickly pushed the morphine into his vein and apologized for letting the suffering get to such a level. I had failed him. His buddy stayed with him, talking to him, consoling him, until the medicine took effect and the soldier's hand relaxed. These two were not in the same unit. They were not wounded in the same part of Iraq. They were brought together and bonded by their wounds.

While in Spain, we experienced the bonding of patients. Those boys had spent seven to ten days together since being injured. They worked together and took care of each other. If someone was unable to walk, a patient who could walk would get food for him. Their injuries made them part of a fraternity. I was fortunate to witness that private brotherhood.

At the end of our twelve days in Spain, we were finally assigned a mission stateside. Stateside missions were incredibly different from flying out of the war zone. At that point, most of the GIs could take care of themselves. If someone on crutches needed help to the bathroom, a battle buddy was there to help. Many of the patients were done with the IV medications and could self-medicate. In contrast to a mission from out of the sand box, the mission stateside was boring. There were no red lights, no combat checklists, and no threats of being shot at.

I had just finished checking on a patient when I saw two patients playing chess. They were older reservists. They did not look like soldiers coming home from war. They looked like two elderly men playing chess on a Sunday afternoon at Point Defiance Park. I could smell the fresh-cut grass of the park when I looked at them. They looked so out of place on a military transport.

I had to get ready for landing in the US. Once again, jet problems caused us to miss our scheduled landing. A fuel leak in Spain delayed takeoff. We did not land in Washington, DC, until twenty-one hours after alert.

A senior officer in dress uniform and an entourage strutted to the ramp and wanted to shake the hand of each patient. We looked at him with disgust. If he would have taken the time to look closely at everyone on board, he would have realized how tired the patients and crew were. As with any war, the further to the rear one got, the more bullshit, paperwork, and politics there were to be dealt with. We finally had to gently push the officer aside so we could get the litter patients off.

The wounded went on to places like Walter Reed and Bethesda hospitals. We cleaned up the plane, turned in narcotics, medical kits, chemical suits, survival equipment, and our weapons. We were in the United States.

Though we were tired, we looked forward to an American hotel, English-language TV with sixty-five channels, and some American food and beer.

Our crew went to the lodging office only to find that no one knew we were crew resting. There were no rooms for us. It took several hours to find a hotel in Alexandria, Virginia. By the time we arrived at our rooms, everything close to the hotel was closed. I was not going to get the Italian baked sub or Redhook beer that I craved. Our first night in the States we ate MREs.

We had the next day off to explore Alexandria. It was weird. I guess I expected to see some overt sign that America was engaged in two major wars (and multiple baby wars in lesser-known countries). Some sign like ration cards for gasoline or Boy Scouts collecting tin cans and old tires for the war effort. Maybe even a blood drive or collecting crutches for the wounded. The day was like any other in peacetime. The news barely mentioned the war.

I was not ready for home and felt out of place in the States. I needed to get back and take care of more patients. I was relieved to get on a plane the next day and return to the conflict.

We left the States and returned to Germany, bypassing England. Mildenhall was closed as an evac stage. The England crews were moved to Germany to consolidate the squadron, another indication that the war was winding down. My taste of life in America stirred memories of home.

# The Rain Brought Me Home

## May 8, 2003

I was supposed to be sleeping. I had to fly a mission the next day but couldn't settle down. It wasn't fear or anxiety that kept me awake that night; not knowing what the next mission would bring kept me up.

I sat barefoot outside and smoked a pipe. A steady stream of smoke drifted over my left shoulder. I could see silver-blue moonlight through the clouds high overhead. Off in the foothills, lightning flashed. The trees were tranquil.

The clouds began to darken, and the moonlight faded to a pale gray. A single drop of warm rain fell on my foot. Gently, several more drops kissed my feet. The raindrops were warm, like blood dripping from an open wound.

I watched the lightning increase in intensity. It was beautiful. The distant rolling thunder sounded like harmony. Daggers of light struck the ground. The pipe smoke stagnated about my face for a moment and then changed direction, pouring over my right shoulder. At that moment, I knew the squall was upon me.

The tree branches began to sway and dance. The wind increased in velocity. The light-colored undersides of the leaves flashed in the streetlights. The rain intensified and dropped in temperature. Random beads of hail ricocheted off the pavement. The thunder shook the glass in the building. I could feel the vibrations in the concrete steps. I watched the storm and thought about how much I was enjoying the moment. I felt completely relaxed watching the supremacy of nature. None of our war machines could match this power.

For a moment, I was lost and daydreaming. I was back in the mountains of Washington . . . and then it was over. Nineteen minutes passed while the thunderstorm grew, lived, and died in front of me. In those nineteen minutes, I was home again and enjoying the outdoors. It was the first time since this conflict had started that I thought seriously of coming home.

The war reminded me to enjoy the simple pleasures in life. I missed sitting on the dock of Spanaway Lake and watching the sunset. I missed talking to my wife while I looked at her. I missed her smile and facial expressions when I said something stupid. I missed the laughter of my friends while we drank at Engine House Number Nine. I missed the feeling of the glacier under my climbing boots, the gentle floating of skis over fresh-fallen snow.

I had something to dream about. I went to sleep.

**May 15, 2003** *US Forces launch Operation Planet X, raiding a village eleven miles south of Tikrit in search of fugitives of the former regime. Two hundred and sixty people are detained, two hundred and thirty of which were released the next day. -CNN*

We had a new nurse that replaced Cathleen. Bob was assigned to us out of Spain. He fit in immediately with the crew. He had been fighting a head cold. He didn't want to report to the flight surgeon and get DNIFed (duties not to include flying). He flew several sorties and endured the ear pain. On our last flight during the descent, the earache was excruciating, and he was grounded. He was diagnosed with barometric-trauma to the eardrums. Fearing we would lose Bob, we begged the CMC to give us twenty-four hours to see if he improved. It was one of the few times a request was granted.

The fifteenth of the month was also my fourth wedding anniversary. I received an e-mail from Jennifer announcing that she was transiting home through Frankfort.

Without knowing for sure when she would pass through Frankfort, I caught the next train to the air base, two hours away. When I arrived at Frankfort, the C-17 stage managers explained that Jennifer's plane would land in six hours to refuel.

My brother was based at the C-17 stage, so the staff recognized the name Hrivnak. They set me up with a van and a private room so I could maximize my time with Jennifer. Eric was gone on a twenty-four hour mission.

Jennifer's transport landed, and I was waiting in the customs holding area. She walked through the gate. All deplaning saw me except her. She finally swung around and made eye contact, but did not recognize me. I had grown a porn star mustache, was tanned, and wore a worn-out desert flight suit. There were bloodstains on my desert boots that I couldn't get out. It had only been a couple of months, but I had aged. She was stunning, with new curly short hair and a deep desert tan.

The shock in her eyes quickly changed to convey how much she loved me. It was one of the best moments of our marriage.

I tried to sneak Jennifer out, but the aerial port troops would not let her leave the customs waiting area. We walked outside on the flight line side and hid inside a hangar door. We had just over an hour alone together, and it was fleeting. The time was a flood of emotion for both of us. We kissed, and it was both arousing and painful. The moments together were tender. We were in love, and it hurt. Reality and the war forced us to leave the privacy of the hangar.

Jennifer slumped to the plane, and the parting was bittersweet. We were happy to see each other, but saying goodbye so quickly almost made the visit not worth it.

Jennifer's group was sent home from the desert after being deployed only six weeks. The conflict was nothing more than glowing embers waiting to be extinguished. Jennifer volunteered to stay in the desert while others who wanted to go home were ordered to remain. The system made no sense.

I also didn't understand why they were being sent home after only six weeks. The rest of us had been deployed for months and wondered why they didn't simply switch. No kind of first in, first out policy had been put in place. Who was managing the war?

I returned by train and taxi to Ramstein within twenty-four hours. Bob was improving. Our crew was removed from the flight schedule until Bob could heal. We were grateful that our crew hadn't been split up.

Bob, like Tom and I, was also a mustang officer. Our enlisted background made it comfortable for us to work together and with our enlisted troops.

The end of April and the first part of May slowed and gave us a false sense that we were going home. Looking back, I'm convinced that the Iraqi generals used the "Mission Accomplished" speech to their tactical advantage. They exploited our artificial victory, stoking the coals we had hoped to smother. It was time for the reorganized Iraqi insurgents to initiate their hit-and-run ambushes. By mid-May, the war was accelerating exponentially. We were not going home. A guerrilla war had started, and it was only our government's bravado that masked the obvious.

The first couple of missions were manageable, but half the squadron was gone. Within two weeks, we were stretched thin and flying continuous missions. The flights blurred. The grinding of gears that shifted the war out of control caught us off guard. I was barely able to record small vignettes of our missions.

# Snapshots of Patients

## May 23

I walked up to a litter patient, and he gave me a look of recognition.

"Hello, it's good to see you again, Captain."

I looked at him for a long time, but couldn't place him. We talked while I assessed. He had a severe GSW to the left arm and multiple leg injuries.

This officer had been establishing some of the new Iraqi leadership. A local warlord hadn't liked what he had had to say at a meeting and had had him personally targeted. After the meeting, where the perceived offense took place, the soldier's convoy was ambushed as they attempted to return to base. He related the story to me.

"We were only about a mile from the base when they hit us with RPG's and small-arms fire. I was hit but was able to return fire. I slumped to the ground and was losing large amounts of blood. I want to stress that it was local Iraqis who came to my aid after the attack."

We played twenty questions with each other, trying to figure out how we might know each other. We finally determined that there was no previous connection. More likely, my twin brother flew this soldier into Iraq—now I was bringing him home.

***

Our plane had an autopilot that was in need of repair. I could look out the window and see the wings slowly rolling up and down. The Dutch roll felt more pronounced in the back of the plane. I placed a vial of medicine on its side and watched it roll with the airplane. To make matters worse, the jet wouldn't cool off after we left the Persian Gulf. Combine the rolling with the desert heat and someone was bound to get sick.

A patient on the top litter tier motioned to me and indicated that he was feeling unsettled. I got there just in time for him to vomit on me and the two patients below him. My medics quickly tried to clean up the emesis, but the bile seeped into the channels and crevices of the cargo floor. The smell rapidly spread through the cabin, and soon others were sick. I was nauseated for the rest of the flight, catching whiffs of dried vomit on my uniform.

I learned my lessons again: Always have barf bags handy. Always anticipate the needs of patients. These soldiers and marines would not ask for help until it was too late. They were conditioned to wait and hold out.

***

A tank recovery commander was engaging a Toyota pick-up truck armed with a mortar tube. They were Iranian regulars that had crossed the border. He told his gunner to fire on the truck with the fifty caliber machine gun. As the young private swung the gun around, he almost knocked the commander off the vehicle. Just then, mortar rounds landed close by, and because he was already off balance, the blast threw the sergeant from the tank.

He had no feeling or movement from the waist down. He was in spinal shock.

By the time he was on our aircraft, he could wiggle some toes on his right foot and he had partial feeling on his right side. I gave him massive doses of Solu-Medrol—a steroid that reduces inflammation.

I reassessed him just after we landed in Germany. He had feeling in both feet. He could wiggle all his toes. He grabbed my hand and wouldn't let go, thanking me profusely for caring and, in his eyes, curing him. Wisps of boyish blond hair covered blue eyes that flowed freely. He was crying for joy as they carried him to the ambulance. Tears welled in my blood-shot orbs as I watched him depart. A drop or two escaped along the dark-circled rings encasing my eyes. But there was no time for emotion; I had forty-nine more patients to get off the plane.

\*\*\*

My new patient was a twenty-two-year-old marine who had been in-country over four months. His grizzled face looked much older than twenty-two. He had survived the battle for Baghdad without a scratch. His job was heavy weapons, mainly the fifty cal.

The marine was driving at night when an oncoming Humvee veered into his lane. He swerved out of the way, narrowly avoiding a head-on collision. The other hummer sheered the side-view mirror off his combat vehicle. Shards of glass sliced through his left eye.

I tried to reach the marine. He was stoic. I tried to get him to talk and open up, but didn't get a single smile. The only thing he told me was that his machine gun got a lot of use. We could care for physical injuries, but his mental wounds were deeper.

\*\*\*

We sat on the sandy, roasting tarmac waiting for a critical patient. The field hospital radioed to us that there was a delay.

The soldier lost his left leg below the knee (from an RPG, the current ambush weapon of choice). There was substantial vascular damage and the surgeons were debating taking the rest of the leg.

They finally decided to delay surgery until we reached Germany. The casualty was brought onto the plane. His face was swollen from all the blood, plasma, and IV fluid transfusions. His skin was pock-marked from shrapnel. No fear in his eyes—just a look of acceptance.

# May 25, 2003

I spoke to the chief nurse about the lack of walk-around bottles. We needed the bottles to breathe if there was a fire or loss of pressurization. She showed no concern.

"If you had a problem, you would only have them on for a few minutes. They are not that important," she told me.

I recalled a mission in 1994, during which our crew lost partial pressurization and had to wear bottles for two hours. I told her about the cockpit fire I experienced in 1993. The crew had to wear the bottles for fifteen minutes because of the smoke and fumes.

There was also the hydraulic fire at Moses Lake in 1992. The pilots lined up on final approach when the cabin filled with smoke. They lost all visibility as the plane touched down. We rolled out on the runway blind. I tried to clear the under-deck and got misting fluid in my eyes from a lack of goggles. My vision was blurred and burning for a week.

She looked confused. She had never had that happen to her. She assumed it never occurred. The colonel decided to provide five bottles. I reminded her that there were seven people on our crew. She responded, "The other two can wear the yellow Dixie Cup masks." Just like the ones you see on passenger planes.

I told her, "The Dixie Cup mask is designed to keep the brain alive, not to keep someone conscious. The mask is also in a fixed location. If we have an in-flight emergency, I will need every one of the seven crewmembers conscious and mobile to take care of the fifty to eighty patients we have on-board."

"Five bottles is all you get." The leadership was willing to compromise safety as long as the mission was accomplished.

We were alerted and once again were missing walk-around bottles. I begged the ground support to find some bottles. As I was pre-flighting for the mission, I noticed blood and vomit on the floor from a previous mission. I looked closer and found dirty needles in the rails of the floor. The crews were tired and hadn't completed all their work. Aircrews were making mistakes. I knew I'd dropped about a dozen used needles on the floor of the plane, never able to find them again. The next mission taught me some humility.

# Be Careful What You Ask For

## May 26, 2003

I finally flew with an old friend, Major Anne Thomas. Annie and I had known each other since meeting during the first Gulf War at Dhahran, Saudi Arabia. Our families spent the summers wakeboarding together. Her husband Dave and I had climbed Mt. Rainier and Mt. Baker, so we knew each other well. Having Annie on the mission was part of the extended military family.

This was our second urgent mission, and the patient load was light, about twenty. The really sick patients were assigned to Annie's critical care air transport team (CCATT). This left me with little to do. My patients were stable and required minor attention. I was frustrated that CCATTs were getting the challenging patients.

Stupid.

I took time to vent a bit with Annie about how her critical care nurses were stealing my job. Annie was sympathetic to my cause. She too felt there wasn't an even distribution of patients between the CCATTs and the evac crews. I went on my way to find something to do, like watching fluid leak from the jet's number three hydraulic system.

We reached cruising altitude and my medic Amara, grabbed my arm and said she believed one of my patients was having trouble. He was a National Guard soldier that had fallen and had a burst fracture in his spine.

The nurse at the field hospital said he was stable and that there shouldn't be any problems. My preflight assessment was normal.

The patient's oxygen level was low, about 80 percent. On the pressurized airplane the saturation level should have been around 94-96 percent. He looked okay, and I asked him how he felt.

"I'm fine, 'cept I can't get comfortable with my back. There's an ache in my lower back."

Treat the patient, not the monitor. I told Amara to get another monitor as I assessed him. I looked at his chest. The rhythmic rise and fall from his lungs moving air was more telling. Air is life. I couldn't hear the heart in-flight, so chest movement was the primary sign. The dead can't move air, though the heart can continue to beat after death.

As I talked to him, he became agitated and anxious in front of me. This was a classic sign of respiratory distress. The second monitor was connected, confirming the readings of the first monitor: this guy wasn't getting air. He had a rapid heart rate of 120 beats per minute (BPM). Giving high-flow oxygen only brought his oxygen level up to 90 percent.

I quickly went though his chart, trying to find a reason for his breathing problem. The guardsman had been stationary for three days. He had received a bolus of IV fluids, and there was no record of urine output. I suspected that he was overloaded with fluid and now had a build-up in the lungs. The ache in his back also suggested pooling of fluid. Because of the jet noise, I couldn't listen to his lungs to confirm this hunch. I checked my altimeter: the cabin altitude was eight thousand feet, which is not good for respiratory distress.

I grabbed the CCATT doctor and reported what I thought was going on. Doc Hart ordered blood gases and lab work. I was surprised. I couldn't do that. He educated me on his team's capabilities. He said to talk to Annie.

I'd just finished complaining to Annie and now I needed her help. She and her respiratory technician, Candice, drew the lab work that confirmed our fears. The patient's blood gasses looked bad, and he had a low potassium level. The doctor gave orders for lasix, a medicine that helps remove excess fluid. He also ordered an IV potassium drip. I didn't have potassium in my kit and had to borrow it from Annie.

Soon the patient pissed 1,200 ccs of fluid and was breathing easier, but he still required an oxygen mask. His heart rate dropped and became irregular. We watched closely. Annie and I took turns caring for him. We balanced the oxygen and meds during the flight. I asked the pilots to drop altitude. We didn't have excess fuel to descend, so the flight engineer brought the cabin altitude down a scant thousand feet. As the flight droned on, the respiratory technician, Candice, tried to wean the patient off oxygen without success. He had to spend the rest of the flight with a mask on.

We landed and got the patient to the hospital. It was the last time I complained about boredom on a flight.

# Snapshots of Aeromedical Evacuation

**May 31, 2003** *About a dozen Iraqi fighters within the Abu Hanifa mosque shoot and toss grenades at soldiers from the US Army 1st Armored Division. The attacks injure two American soldiers; the return fire kills two Iraqis. -CNN*

We continue to find ways to blow of stress. Robert shaves his head to protest the war. I follow his lead and shave my head and B-grade mustache.

Chief master sergeant Dillinger gave us the keys to his room so a transiting crew from the desert could unwind. The MCD, major Kathleen Flarity narrated life downrange compared to Germany. Kathleen is a vivacious blond and was tent-mates with Jennifer in Oman. She provides colorful stories of living with my wife. Jennifer nicknamed her the energizer bunny because of her unfaltering spirit and drive. It's a reminder that I have a spouse.

By the time chief Dillinger was off shift, an impromptu party was in full swing in his quarters. The carpet was wet from spilled drinks and empty bottles are tossed out the window and litter the grass. We consumed all his beer and had a contest to see how many nurses could be stuffed in his shower. The antics mask that the next mission is just a phone call away. The long duty days continue to chip at our long term health. The mounting sleep deprivation warps memory. Flights are remembered as a window blind opened briefly, exposing quick views of the life of a flyer.

***

We took off at night in time to see the moon rise. The moon was huge, close—you could reach through the cockpit window and grab it. Its rich glow was the color of Sicilian blood oranges.

***

We entered the AOR airspace in time to see the sunrise. There were no clouds—just the dirty, ugly haze of the Middle East. Our eyes were dry and tired from the flight down. Daggers of sunlight stabbed through the haze to pierce them . . .

***

Some days we drank until we forgot what we did. Some days we drank so we forgot what we were going to do. Some days we drank so we didn't think about home. Some days we were too tired to drink.

***

On a flight downrange, the plane was stuffed with whole blood that had to be kept cold. The cargo compartment was a balmy forty-three degrees Fahrenheit. It was cold enough that sleep was just a fantasy. We landed in the desert, and the cargo doors opened. The heat melted our strength and we wished for the cold.

\*\*\*

We flew a mission with no combat casualties. All of our patients were involved in accidents or had medical conditions. We treated many who had been in vehicle accidents. Treating noncombat injuries was easier to manage.

The volume of patients kept increasing. An average channel mission had fifty to seventy patients. Just when we thought the war might be over, a bomb went off, a small unit got ambushed, and we received a fresh load of wounded. Thankfully, our evac planes usually did not transport the dead. Our mission was to fly the living.

\*\*\*

No one wanted to be grounded. Clipping the wings of a flyer is like taking a toy away from a child. The military did not call it being grounded. That was too harsh. You were DNIF.

Many of us had injuries or sicknesses that could get us grounded. Most didn't say anything. It was common to see someone self-medicating to get through a mission. It was not uncommon to see someone using Bengay or icing a tired muscle or strained back after lifting dozens of patients. Rarely were there skinny combat casualties on litters.

If you were DNIF, you were assigned a ground job. It was punishment for getting sick. You didn't get to fly again until someone else got sick to take your place. Flyers didn't like ground jobs, but they were a necessity.

\*\*\*

Maintenance continued to be a problem with the C-141. The mechanics tried their best. The planes were old, and there were few spare parts. It was sad to see the slumped shoulders of a mechanic who had done all he could and still the plane would not fly.

\*\*\*

We left one broken plane and moved our stuff onto the spare. This was called "tail-swapping." Once on our new plane, we had taxied about a hundred feet when the plane suddenly stopped.

The scanner deplaned and looked underneath the aircraft for skid marks. The plane was telling the crew that the anti-skid system had failed. This happened five or six times. Taxi a few hundred feet, stop, and the scanner looked for skid marks. They finally fixed the problem—nine hours after the original plane's scheduled takeoff time.

Can you imagine flying on a commercial flight stateside and having that happen? I was losing my confidence in these old birds.

\*\*\*

I was waiting in line for a beer when I noticed a guy with an airborne tab on his desert uniform. He was from the 503rd Airborne Regiment. I asked him if he had made the combat drop into Northern Iraq. He said yes and that it was a memorable experience. He told me he absolutely loved jumping out of the C-17 transport jet.

I asked him if they took any ground fire. He said, "I saw flashes while under canopy, they might have been people taking pictures. The people of Northern Iraq gave a really warm welcome. They love Americans up north. They were throwing flowers at us."

***

My twin brother Eric lands in Germany after a twenty-six hour mission. We share martinis as Eric describes flying tactical assaults in the C-17. "There's no manual yet on how to enter combat with this new plane; it's word of mouth training. I fly near red-line at three hundred and thirty knots and a minimum combat altitude of one hundred fifty to three hundred feet. The subtle changes in altitude prevent wing flash and make it tougher for an Iraqi gunner to get a bead on us. The best part is popping up just before the runway, throwing the landing gear and flaps out, and landing before anyone has time to react. We land on taxiways in Baghdad because the runways are cratered from the bombing. Some of the most enjoyable flying I've ever done, a real guilty pleasure."

I start to explain the life of medevac compared to being a pilot. After rambling for minutes, I realize my brother was sound asleep supine on a picnic table. He was exhausted from the extended crew day. I finish his drink and left him basking in the afternoon sun. It is the only time we see each other during the deployment. Brief contacts like this are the norm for flyers as they are turned for another mission.

***

Our living and work conditions had improved and Germany was now home. Many of us had private lodging rooms on base. We stored equipment in our rooms instead of toting everything we owned on each mission. We had trimmed the amount of combat equipment we carried. Our chemical bags were smaller, and I had not worn a pistol in over a month.

Our rooms were above the standards of many hotels (and beat living in a tent in the sand). We had hot showers, real beds, and did laundry. Our rooms had refrigerators, microwaves, coffeepots, and of course the German porn.

In crew rest we ate German food, drank dark German beer, and looked at Arian women. It was life in the air force, if privileged to be on flight status.

It was exactly two months since I flew my first medical evacuation mission for Operation Iraqi Freedom. In the last sixty days, our crew had flown twenty-five sorties and evacuated 202 patients. The *Air Force Times* reported last week that over 1,500 patients have been evacuated during Operation Iraqi Freedom.

# The Month of June:
# BLOODY, HOT, and
# TIRED

A month after George Bush had declared major combat operations over, we still held onto the President's words that the fighting was over. I was proud of President Bush. It was comforting to see him in our uniform and supporting his military. I thought we were close to being done. I fell for the whole theatrical act.

His words impacted military readiness in the desert. None of us knew that at the time.

Thirty days after his speech, a trend developed in the patients we were transporting. We were inundated with noncombat casualties. Troops were reporting to the field aid stations with a multitude of complaints. Some had genuine injuries or conditions that they had ignored until major combat had been declared over. Many were weary of the desert and wanted to go home. I think all of them felt after the "Mission Accomplished" speech that they had done their part and that it was time for home. We saw an increase in nontraumatic cases, pregnancies, and psych patients. Coupled with this was the increased accident rate from sleep deprived GIs fatigued from combat. There were also a number of malingerers wanting a ticket out. The war was only to last six weeks. That's what Donald Rumsfeld had promised. There were no in-country regional hospitals, so routine patients were evaced to Germany for treatment.

The military certainly conveyed that the war was ending. We started packing our stage base at Sicily. We had thirteen crews remaining to cover the intercontinental missions. At any given time, two crews were down, leaving us with eleven crews to actually fly. We thought home was within reach.

The month of June changed all of that. The summer heat hit with full force. Dehydration and heat stroke became a real problem. The tarmac at Camp Wolf averaged one hundred and fourteen degrees, with eighty to ninety percent humidity. Increasing desert winds would slam gritty sand into every exposed orifice, whether it was man or machine. And the Iraqis fought back.

At first there were sporadic ambushes, many with RPGs. As the month progressed, the attacks became more sophisticated. Troops were now killed and wounded by remote improvised explosive devices (IEDs), followed by RPGs or a hail of AK-47 gunfire. June was the first time I had heard the term IED. The wounds from the IED's were devastating, unlike anything we had seen before. Advanced weaponry smuggled from Iran increased the casualty rate.

Aircraft were getting shot at too. The C-130 medevacs were taking ground fire. A fellow nurse sent a picture of her plane with the tire shot out from a high caliber machine gun. There were reports of SAMs launched. So far none of our C-141s or C-17s had been hit, but there was an increase of flare use from the defensive systems.

Coupled with that, our equipment was war-weary. Maintenance problems increased. Planes would break, and the crews would get stuck, unable to complete their missions. This made it harder for us to cover the evacs. On some days, there were no legal crews to sit on BRAVO alert to stand by for urgent missions. Our medical equipment also exhibited signs of failure.

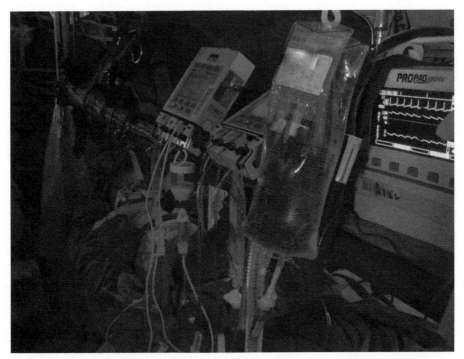

**Two IV pumps on far left for one critical patient. Heart monitor is on right side.
Patient is on a ventilator.**

Our IV pumps failed. Oftentimes we would not have enough
pumps for the patients. The pumps could handle three lines
at once. Sometimes I would flow meds through a pump to two
different patients. This was a risky procedure, because it was easy to
gets the lines crossed and deliver the wrong flow rate to the wrong
patient. Or one patient could have three IVs running at once, and
then I would have to flow other patients' IVs the old-fashioned
way, by counting the drops. You had to keep an eye on the drops,
because changes in aircraft pressurization could change the rate
or stop the IV from flowing. By mid-June, at least one channel of
the pump would not function. The medical equipment that had
been held in war-readiness storage for years didn't hold up to the
rigors of combat medicine. June would be the worst month during
our deployment. History would show that each subsequent June

would increase the volume of the dead and wounded. We had the first visceral taste of extended combat.

# June 1, 2003

We landed in Kuwait at 0400. Bobby Pederson and I were standing on the ramp of the plane watching the massive cargo doors open.

I looked over at Bob. The years had been kind to him. He was in his early fifties with Robert Redford hair and looking about thirty-five. Only the crow's feet around his eyes hinted of age. He had nearly three decades of experience as an engineer and knew his jet.

As we watched the doors open, the right door continued past the travel stop. There was a noticeable grinding of gears and machinery, followed by a *klunk*. The pedal door then dropped, hanging freely. Bobby looked at me and said, "The gear box is toast. They don't make the parts anymore. The only place we can get the part is probably out of the bone yard in Arizona. We better look for a plane to tail-swap."

The bone yard Bobby referred to was Davis-Monthan AFB in the moisture-free Arizona desert. The military stored retired aircraft there, preserving them for future use. Sometimes the planes ended up being target drones. Sometimes they were sold to third-world countries. In the case of the aging C-141, the retired planes were being stripped of their parts and chopped into pieces.

Bobby informed the rest of the crew that we needed another plane. We packed up our stuff. The pilots walked to base operations to call home. Even though we were in a war zone, the crew still needed to report to TACC in Illinois. While this was going on, a C-5 crew chief came out to the plane to have a discussion with Bobby. The crew chief told Bobby that he used to service C-141s and thought he might be able to fix the plane. Bobby said, "Not a chance, but go ahead and have a look if it makes you feel better."

**Stranded in Kuwait. Right side pedal door is broken and hanging low.
We are unable to close the doors to fly.**

In the meantime, the base transit maintenance, operations, and the duty officers in Illinois wanted to fix the plane. There was a C-141 on the ramp that we could swap to, but everyone else had made up their minds that they could fix the plane. Bobby knew the Starlifter was hard broke, and that was good enough for me. Hours passed as the pilots conversed with TACC and the mechanics attempted to fix the plane. By then, the sun was high above the horizon, and the temp soared over 105 degrees. The radiant heat off of the tarmac increased the temperature. We baked inside the cargo compartment.

I knew that I was dehydrated. I could actually feel the dried salt of my body rub against my flight suit, irritating my armpits, groin, and the backsides of my knees. White sweat stains formed like baloney rings on the armpits of my Nomex.

**Waiting for jet to be repaired. Robert (Foo-Foo) and I
shaved our heads in protest of the war.**

The mechanics finally decided the same thing Bobby had told them four hours ago. The plane was *hard* broke. TACC asked if we could load the patients, then manually close the pedal doors. They wanted us to use cargo straps to hold the doors in place for a one-time flight to Germany.

I thought about that for a minute. We only had about three hours left on the ground before we busted our crew duty day. We had fifty-five patients to load. Twenty-two of them were on litters. Once the patients were loaded, it would take an hour to manually close the doors and set the rated five thousand-pound straps in place. With the doors manually locked in place, we would not be able to open them without tearing the internal guts of the jackscrews apart. There was also no guarantee that the broken gearbox and straps would hold the pedal doors in place as we flew at over five hundred miles per hour at thirty-five thousand feet.

I asked the pilots on the phone with TACC how we would get fifty-five patients off the plane. The pilots asked the question to TACC. TACC responded that we could use the troop doors. The troop doors are at the back of the aircraft and stand six feet above the ground. They are normally only used by airborne troops on a parachute drop. On the ground, a specially made ramp was needed to use the door. I knew there was no ramp available in either Kuwait or Germany. We would then have to use six people and an overhead lift the remove the litter patients one at a time. It would take a couple hours to get twenty-two litters out the troop door. It was considered an emergency procedure. Our remaining thirty-three walking wounded would have to exit the steep ladder of the crew entrance door. Many of the patients were medicated with narcotics and would have difficulty using the ladder.

I discussed this with the other two nurses on our crew. We were in agreement that the risks involved and the extra time that the patients would have to sit in the baking airplane were excessive. So, we reported to TACC that we were not accepting the jet in the interest of patient safety. They needed to get another transport, something Bobby had decided five hours ago. Everyone finally agreed.

I asked about the spare C-141, and it was already taxiing down the runway. A radio call kept it from taking off and brought the plane back to where we were parked.

As the day stretched, the heat on the tarmac amplified. We then had to move off the broken jet and tail-swap to the new jet. Everyone available pitched in. The deconfiguration and reconfiguration of a C-141 was a painful process. The equipment was old and had been abused. Over decades of use, some of the stuff didn't work correctly. Flight gloves and hands were easily torn on tie-down rings. The oxygen and electrical lines had to be removed. The litter stanchions were stripped and stowed in overhead compartments of the plane. They were heavy and had to be manhandled into position. In our rush to move, an overhead stanchion broke free and clubbed Major Tom in the head. He sweated and bled freely from his forehead. A quick bandage and Tom was back to work.

The thousand pounds of medical supplies and combat gear had to be moved by hand to the new airplane. It was hard work, and the heat added a physical weight on our backs. The cargo floor became slick from free-flowing sweat. Our tan flight suits were soaking wet, dark brown. We looked like we just stepped out of the shower with our clothes on. The heat accentuated the smell of our bodies and the chemical toilets on the plane. The smell of the Middle East also permeated the air. Sand covered everything. I drank two thousand ccs of water from my Camelbak, but I never pissed.

The tail-swap normally takes two hours. We were ready to receive patients in an hour. We left Bobby behind with his front-end crew to stay with the broken plane. But then there was the question of fuel.

The plane we had taken had extra fuel onboard because it was flying to Germany empty. They did not have any cargo weight, so they tankered fuel. We were loaded with eighty-three souls on board, plus baggage, field gear, and the weapons of the wounded. The plane was technically over its gross weight. I discussed this with the loadmaster. It would take hours to defuel the airplane. At that rate, we would bust our duty day and have to spend the night. The loadmasters and engineers went over the data to crunch the numbers. We knew from the first Gulf War that the plane could carry more weight and use data tables known as war weights. The plane was restricted from war weights for Iraqi Freedom. It was too old and suffered from fatigue. We knew the plane could handle the weight. No one wanted to defuel. No one wanted to offload the patients. We all wanted to complete the mission. The data was fudged using war weights, the numbers adjusted on paper; we were then magically back within weight limits.

The aircrew started the engines and slowly moved out of parking. Extra power was needed to maneuver the heavy *Starlifter.* As we lumbered down the taxiway, the aircrew and medical crew completed last-minute checklist items. Patients were secured in place for takeoff. Last minute morphine was given. The air-conditioning didn't dent the desert heat or the eighty-three sweating bodies. Bottled water that has been heated on the tarmac was passed out. It offered no relief.

The line-up check was completed as we were cleared for takeoff at 1045. Though major combat was declared over, the aircrew still manned the troop door windows looking for missiles, ready to punch off flares.

We had been on the ground for seven hours working in the desert sun. Now the treatment of patients and real work began.

I was on the headset and listened to the pilots discuss the weight of the aircraft. They applied the brakes and spooled the engines to full power. This was known as a maximum total rated thrust takeoff (TRT). Normally when the brakes are released, the plane lunges forward. This time the overweight jet crept at a slow roll. I time-hacked my watch. At thirty seconds we were still rolling down the runway. At forty seconds the copilot called rotate on the interphone. The pilot pulled back on the yoke, and nothing happened. At forty-five seconds, the landing gear let go of the runway and the jet engines clawed for sky. The pilots gently banked, and I could see out the troop window that we are very close to the ground. The C-141 was a pregnant cow, yet it managed to stay airborne.

An hour into the flight, we had still not reached the cool air of the stratosphere. The interior of the plane was a furnace. The aircrew realized that we were too heavy to reach our assigned altitude. They called and coordinated a lower altitude for cruising. We had to stay down until enough fuel was burned off to lighten the jet. The result was a bumpier, warmer flight for the first four hours of the mission.

I don't have clear recollections of the rest of the flight. It had been days since I had had a decent night of sleep. My body had no idea what time zone it was in.

I recall a patient passing out in the bathroom with dehydration. Patients and crew desperately needed liquids. We landed in Germany at 1800 hours after an eight-hour flight. A tailwind got us on the ground before we busted our day. It took several hours to transfer the patients, clean the airplane, and store our equipment. I went to the CMC, turned in mission paperwork, and called TACC with a verbal mission report.

As I was leaving, I asked the cell if my crew could sleep in tomorrow and get some laundry done. "No way, you need to report for duty at 0700. Lots of work to be done," the CMC reported. There was no point in arguing. We got a ride back to our rooms after turning in weapons.

Jeremy jumped in the shower while I made martinis. Tom stopped by for one. We were too tired to talk. The heat had worn me out and we were not acclimated to it. The wounded asked for blankets when the temperature dropped below ninety degrees in the plane. They were used to the 110-degree temps. The constant change of continental climates affected us as much as the time zone changes.

Jeremy shuffled out of the shower and turned on cartoons. We couldn't stand to watch the news anymore and the drivel about the war. Cartoons were a good escape. MTV was also low-stress entertainment.

I was entranced by a new band called "Evanescence." The female vocalist's haunting voice and disturbing lyrics were reminiscent of our war. The music made me consider the war and what I was doing was futile. No matter how hard I worked, there was always another load of bodies to bring out of the desert. I turned the channel, looking for humor.

An old *M\*A\*S\*H* rerun was on. The more we watched *M\*A\*S\*H*, the more we realized it was the medical military. The insanity of it.

Hawkeye created an imaginary friend, Captain Tuttle, to take care of his problems. I decided Captain Tuttle would take care of my future problems.

I showered, and Tom left to sleep. There had been discussion about staying up to watch German porn at eleven. Another martini and I was asleep by eight. But it was not good sleep. I tossed and turned, too exhausted to enjoy it.

The next morning, our crew met at 0645 for ground support. We sat on the curb waiting for a van to pick up the crew or I should say, pick up the dead. We looked like hell. Small talk was made and no one slept well. Bob, our newest nurse on the crew, managed to pop off a few jokes about sex. Bob kept the mood light and told stories. His soft-spoken voice and animated face was perfect for storytelling. He was a tall, jolly man.

At 0745 there was still no van for us. I called and the van picked us up at eight. They forgot we were working.

We dragged ourselves to the supply hangar and restocked our medical kits. IV needles, bandages, tape, tubing . . . it was routine now. We inspected the heart monitor and IV pumps. Charged batteries and readied for the next load. After a couple of hours of work, I asked to be released. CMC told us they had nothing going on that day, but they didn't want to release us, so we went to lunch.

We borrowed a van to drive to the base exchange (BX) to eat. The seven of us sat quietly and poked at our meals. I spotted the chief nurse walking our way and told everyone not to make eye contact.

She eyed us and strolled over. She was a taller woman with blond hair, fit and probably attractive ten years ago. I referred to her as the chief nurse because that's how she had introduced herself when we first landed in England back in March. By June, she was calling herself the director of operations (DO). I had never been in a unit where the chief nurse was the same as the DO. They have two very distinct and different jobs within a medical flying squadron. It didn't matter what she called herself.

The chief nurse sat next to me and asked how things were going. I didn't hesitate.

"We are tired. We're behind on sleep and can't get caught up. I'm concerned that we are going to have an accident. We bust our duty day on a regular basis, working our asses off when we fly. I'm also worried about maintenance. The planes are exceptionally unreliable. It's not safe, and someone is going to get hurt." As I spoke to her, I could tell she wasn't listening. She was formulating an answer in her mind.

She responded, "I'm not worried about you busting duty days. The reality is you are only working for the period of time that you have patients onboard, which is roughly eight hours. So the fact of the matter is, what you're doing isn't any different than working an eight- to ten-hour shift in a hospital. As far as sleep goes, you get to sleep the whole way down into the AOR. Remember, you're an augmented crew. You have seven people to care for those patients. You're lucky to have a seven-person crew. You can thank me for insisting that the crew has seven people on it."

I thought my mind was going to explode. Bob was so mad he got up from the table and walked away. So did one of the medics. Jeremy had a piece of hamburger in his mouth, unable to chew at the words he heard.

My mind spun as I thought about the last mission. So working in 114-degree heat, tail-swapping an airplane did not count as work? Tearing a plane down did not count as work? And had she ever tried to sleep on a pallet flying into a combat zone? The patients were under our care from the time they came out to the plane until they were loaded in the ambulance at Germany. It was never eight hours. It was often twelve to fourteen hours. There were times that we loaded them onto the bus and had to continue providing care. I was furious. I had never had to wear a flak vest or helmet when working back in the States. I had never had to split fifty to eighty-five patients between three nurses and four medics. And these were not just stable medical patients. Many of them were traumatic *combat injuries. Flying at 35,000 feet with an assload of wounded out of a combat zone is not like being in a stateside hospital.*

I tried to formulate in my mind how to respond to such a statement. I tried to remember that she was a superior officer.

Tom was mad, but he could see I was boiling. He was the more levelheaded of the two of us. He was better at tact than I was. He tried to defuse the conversation, but my voice was loud with an insubordinate tone.

"Why don't you come fly with us sometime, Colonel? And you can see what it is like. Why not fly with us on these old tubs that are ready to fall out of the sky! When was the last time we had a plane take off on time? How many planes do we have broken on the ramp right now?" She responded that she was going to fly a mission. I told her to make sure she flew with us so I could point out to her what it is really like. And then I stormed off.

That conversation with the chief nurse blew morale. The crew was convinced that our squadron leadership couldn't give a shit about us.

Back to the warehouse and still no work. So after sitting around another two hours, the CMC released us and put us into predeparture crew rest. We were going back out.

# June 4, 2003

We were alerted for another mission to Kuwait and then on to Spain. The operations at Ramstein AB were haphazard and rarely flowed. We reported to operations for our briefing. There were no pilots. I made a few calls only to find out the front-end crew hadn't been alerted. So we were already off schedule. We started loading the plane and were told to leave room for two cargo pallets. We were setting up litters when the ground loaders told us they actually had three pallets. We broke litter stanchions down and moved them forward. Another loader came out, and we then had a wheeled nitrogen cart. So we again moved the medical setup forward. The pilots finally showed. The loadmaster was arguing over the nitrogen cart. There was no documentation to carry the cart with pressurized liquid nitrogen bottles on the plane. The ground crew argued that it was needed to repair a C-141 in Kuwait.

The plane turned out to be the C-141 that we left with the broken pedal door. The plane had been sitting so long that nitrogen was needed to pump up the struts on the landing gear. The loadmaster would not budge. With his arms crossed, he said, "If the cart is not properly prepared for flight, it's not going."

That was fine by me. I didn't want to fly with pressurized frozen liquid.

We missed our takeoff window. It was now German quiet hours, which started at 2200 hours. Special permission was granted to takeoff, finally, at 2235. A fine would be paid to the German authorities for the late night noise. Five hours of unloading and reloading just to get one airplane airborne. The commercial airlines would be bankrupt if they operated like the air force. This was normal out of Ramstein. There was no sense of urgency to get evac planes in the air.

On the flight down, I talked to the passengers. They were air force tactical air control parties (TACPs): forward air controllers. They lived with the army and directed planes for close air support. They were on their way home when the air force ordered them back to Iraq. This proved that the war was heating up and that we were not prepared for these increased guerilla attacks. These guys were coming back to call airstrikes on the insurgents. I felt sorry for them. They were so close to home.

Bobby had remained in Kuwait to fix the broken plane. He was mad that we didn't bring the nitrogen cart. In one way of looking at it, I technically screwed my friend for the sake of safety.

"This is costing you a martini and a German dinner," Bobby lamented with raised fist. It was a few more nights in the desert for his crew.

We loaded thirty-six patients. There was a delay waiting for a C-130 to bring patients from Baghdad. Two patients were older reservists with chest pain. There had been an increase of older Guard and Reserve military being evacuated for chest pain.

The C-130 arrived, and I tried to coordinate an engine running onload (ERO). But the local Kuwaiti authorities wouldn't allow it. A normal two-hour ground time was stretched to five.

We were airborne and off to Spain and back to Fleet Hospital 8. At debriefing, we were notified that there was a bottleneck of evac crews at Rota. Three medical missions were landing a week, but there was only one outbound flight. A bunch of crews were waiting in front of us for a mission. The CMC kept us on the hook, and we had to check in each day. We ended up with five days off on the coast of Spain.

# Sunny Rota Spain

## June 6-11, 2003

Just what our crew needed: a little time off to recharge and get regular rest and exercise. We were no longer staying in the sea huts but had been moved downtown to the Hotel de Playa. It was a resort on the beach. I could sit on my balcony and watch topless European women tan their soft, smooth skin. I was happy in Rota, Spain. Suddenly on the beach, the nightmarish war had been temporarily purged from my brain.

I spent the days running on the beach and swimming in the ocean. At night we would go out and eat fresh fish and garlic shrimp. Sangria flowed freely.

I tried to call Jennifer without success. We kept missing each others call. There were days when my wife and home seemed like a sort of past life that no longer existed. Reality was measured one twenty four hour mission at a time.

At the end of the five days, I felt rested enough to face my obligation. I could have easily stayed. I was losing interest in war.

# June 12, 2003

We were alerted to fly to Sicily, normally recycling through Germany. There was a shortage of crews at the forward stage, so we went directly to Sigonella. At report, a composite crew was there from the air force supporting the fleet hospital. I noticed immediately that they did not have any combat equipment with them. I asked their MCD, "Where's your downrange gear? Where are your survival vests, Kevlar, and weapons?"

He stated, "The chief nurse said we could fly a training mission to Sigonella and then come home. We aren't permitted to go downrange."

It was midnight, and I was already irritable. I felt the acid churn in my stomach. "Are you guys nuts? We're short crews. Once we get to Sig, they are going to turn you for a combat mission. We need everyone that can fly the line."

He responded, "I'm just following the orders of the chief nurse." These guys were flying to get their flight pay and were going to get screwed for it. There was no point in arguing. God forbid an air force officer think for himself and disobey a stupid order. We took off from Rota at 0200 and landed at Sigonella at 0500.

The summer sun was starting to rise. I could see that all the snow had melted on Mt. Etna. Jimmy, a medic from my first crew, met us at the plane. He told the composite crew that they were launching downrange. He explained, "We had back-to-back urgent missions. We don't have a single crew available on the island. I need your crew to go now."

I glared a look at the MCD that said, *I told you so*. Jimmy was dumbfounded when the MCD explained they had no combat gear and were ordered by the chief nurse to return to Spain. Jimmy looked at our crew with sad eyes.

"I'm sorry that I have to do this to you. You guys get minimum crew rest and fly out this evening."

Our crew got to bed at 0900. There was no air-conditioning. Sicilian laborers were remodeling the hotel while we lay in bed. The noise and summer heat made it difficult to sleep. I managed a two-hour nap. Jimmy alerted us at 1900 hours. He grabbed my arm as we were leaving and leaned in so no one else could hear. "They are closing the stage down and operations are moving to Kuwait. The hotel staff is hosting an all you can eat and drink party before we leave." Jimmy knew the real news was the party that our crew was going to miss. Operating out of Kuwait was secondary.

I remember fragments of flight. We skipped through four countries and two continents in a day and a half. My flight logbook states that there were sixty-two patients onboard the flight from Camp Wolf to Germany. I made a note, "Busy during entire flight . . . typical bullshit when landing at Ramstein."

The days of Spanish rest were wiped clean. Thankfully, no patients were hurt due to sleep deprivation.

**Drawing up antibiotics to treat dirty combat wounds during an exceptionally busy flight.**

# Unexplained Patients

*There are known knowns. These are things we know
that we know. There are known unknowns. That is to say,
there are things that we know we don't know. But
there are also unknown unknowns. There are
things we don't know we don't know.*

*- Donald Rumsfeld*

## June 16, 2003

*Nine US soldiers are wounded battling pockets of Iraqi
resistance - CNN*

During the surge of wounded evaced, patients were treated that
had unusual injuries.

We transported several patients on ventilators with
unexplained respiratory illnesses. It looked like pneumonia, but
the docs weren't sure of the cause. Eleven GIs had died from
it, and over a hundred had been diagnosed. We were leery of
treating these patients because there were no special precautions.
Was it contagious?

On one mission, we transported two patients with radiation exposure. The story was that they had opened Iraqi fifty-five gallon drums and found radioactive waste inside. We were evacing them for radiation sickness. Where did the drums come from?

Several patients we transported had thyroid problems of unknown origin. These troops had been involved with clearing disabled Iraqi armor. The Iraqi tanks and personnel carriers had been hit by depleted uranium rounds. Was the dust from the depleted uranium causing the thyroid problems?

One patient I had had blisters on his ankles, feet, hands, and wrists. He was a navy Seabee that operated a large bulldozer. Seabee's were combat construction teams. He was ordered to collapse old Iraqi trenches. After the job was done, he rinsed off the bulldozer. His hands and feet got wet. Soon after, he broke out into a blistered rash. The blisters looked just like exposure to mustard gas, a chemical weapon. Was there mustard gas in Iraq?

Another patient complained to me about supply problems. I could empathize because of our own supply shortages. He was distraught because he witnessed a comrade die of heat stroke and dehydration.

"We got as many MREs as we wanted, but there was a shortage of bottled water. You would only get two bottles of water a day. With the shortage of water, the body could only handle eating one MRE."

"Did you have any local water?"

"They did bring out water buffalos (storage tank) of local water. They said it was treated, but no one trusted drinking the local."

This soldier was mad about the supply problems and gave little concern towards his own injury. Why was the most powerful army in the world having supply problems? Oh yeah, we had been promised a six-week war that would pay for itself in six months. Thanks, Dick Cheney.

As the war dragged, we treated more civilians with combat injuries. The American military was so small that civilian contractors were used to fill the gaps. They were vets doing the same job they performed in the military, but at much higher salaries. The civilians were wounded and killed. They were not listed on the WIA or KIA rosters. They were awarded no Purple Heart or VA disability for their combat injuries. They received no recognition for losing their lives. They were mercenaries.

On rare occasions, our squadron transported foreign nationals and prisoners of war (POWs). On one mission, they brought us a wounded civilian Pakistani. There were questions and confusion on the ground about whether to load him on the plane. Finally, some litter-bearers brought him. I looked at him with scrutiny. He was dirty and had two external fixators to hold bones in place that had been shattered by rifle fire. He was scared and in pain. He had never been on an American military jet.

Fear and prejudice overcame me as I examined him. I didn't trust him because he looked like the enemy. I searched him, looking for weapons. He grunted in pain as I patted him down. The only time I searched an American soldier was when he came right from the combat line to us. We would find weapons on American soldiers who had not been properly disarmed. The ones who smelled of gunpowder and still wore their shredded desert uniforms were routinely searched. The ground medics, at times overwhelmed by wounded, did not have an opportunity to strip them of their weapons or change them into hospital gowns.

I asked for ID. He spoke little English and didn't understand. I pulled out my own ID card, pointed to me and then to the card. With his good arm he reached under his shirt. I was nervous. He was taking too long. Instinctively, I rested a hand on my holstered Beretta. Though I had searched him, I did not trust him. I thought about what I would do if he pulled a weapon, perhaps a knife or grenade. I thought about whether I could actually draw and shoot him. The thought of shooting someone had never occurred to me.

I was as nervous as he was. We were both sweating. I undid the flap to the holster.

His hand slid out from under his shirt and produced a laminated card. I grabbed the card but kept my right hand on the gun. The ID card was clearly handmade and poorly laminated. One of the English words was misspelled. It didn't look like an authentic ID card. Our eyes locked, and we could both read each other's fear.

Just then, the medics boarded the plane.

"There's been a mistake. This patient is not cleared to Germany." With few details, they unloaded the stretcher. I tucked the ID in his shirt pocket. Though he had injuries that required surgery in Germany, he would not be leaving the desert. Our eyes remained locked as they carried him off. He looked so afraid and in pain. My eyes said I was sorry.

I concluded that he was not the enemy. He was a poor Pakistani that traveled to Iraq to make money and got caught in the crossfire. The Middle East was flooded with third-world nationals looking for work that paid substantially more than work in their poor rural villages. There was such a rush to get services into Iraq that proper ID cards and documentation were rare. There was no infrastructure to support the newly "liberated" country.

I let my own prejudice and fear fail him as a nurse. I never gave him morphine or cared for him as a patient. He had serious injuries and was no threat to our crew.

I reflected on that moment he handed me the ID card. What if he had been the enemy and handed me a grenade instead? Could I have shot him? I had limited training for combat and extensive training and experience in saving lives. I was not certain I could actually draw a weapon and shoot another human being. It was far easier to think it than to actually do it.

# June 21, 2003

We got onboard the C-141 with tail number 181—the pig of the fleet. It was regularly down for repairs and had a reputation for in-flight gremlins. Fliers are superstitious about aircraft. Planes develop personalities. This one was known for its bad persona.

181 had been neglected on the ramp so long that equipment had been cannibalized. We had no MA-1 walk-around bottles for the med crew. If we had a rapid decompression, we would don the walk-around bottle to breathe portable oxygen. There were also no oxygen masks or patient life jackets for the litter patients. We complained about this, the equipment did not show, and we had to leave without required emergency gear.

As we buttoned up the plane, Jimmy poked his head in the crew hatch. He was now in Germany from Sicily. His eyes were blood red, not just blood shot. Jimmy sheepishly explained, "The going away party at Sigonella was one for the ages. I got exceptionally drunk from the open bar. I've been vomiting so violently that I burst the blood vessels in my eye balls." Jimmy looked possessed and hung-over. The engines started and Jimmy was gone. The war was fleeting moments of contact with friends.

181 didn't let us down. It developed a fuel flow problem during taxi. The crew chiefs feverously worked on repairs. We missed our slotted takeoff time and lumbered on to the Middle East.

Seventy-one patients out of Kuwait. The plane was packed. There was no room to move or breath. I knew how the claustrophobic felt. I was beginning to dislike being in crowds or confined places.

To one patient I paid special attention. He was a medic assigned to Camp Wolf. Until last week, he and his driver had brought us patients. They had recently been sent to Baghdad. He had been transporting a casualty in a medical Humvee marked with big red crosses when the bad guys fired an RPG at the back of the ambulance. The rocket traveled through the rear and exploded in the driver's compartment, killing his driver and friend. The medic was wounded by shrapnel and burned from the blast.

I feared that one of my friends would come onto the aircraft, wounded on a litter. This was the closest I came to knowing a casualty. Though we were not friends, working together had established a connection. The medic had the thousand-yard stare.

A fully loaded plane with combat and noncombat patients.

"I am sorry about your friend."

A nod of acknowledgement.

They were empty words as I searched the sorrow on his face. He was a young troop, but with the shrapnel marks on his face and the memories in his eyes, he was old.

I knew it was easy to fix his physical wounds, so I told him, "You know, you are going to be physically okay. You're a medic. . . you know about PTSD. Make sure you talk to someone when you get to the States. Expect nightmares and difficulty sleeping from this. It's not an easy thing to deal with losing a friend."

He nodded.

On flights downrange, we were bringing in replacement troops. The young E-1s to E-3s (junior enlisted) had looks of fear and excitement as we headed in-country. When we brought them out as wounded, their excited adolescent faces were gone.

Gray hair caught my eye. The soldier was an older man with a large, gray cowboy mustache. He was a chief warrant officer (CWO) with master army aviator wings and a 101st Airborne patch. I leaned into him and yelled, "What the hell is an old man like you doing in a war zone?"

He responded, "I've been retired for twelve years and they recalled me. I had twenty-three years in the army and they brought me back. No retraining, the green machine threw me right back in the Blackhawk as a co-pilot."

"What brings you on the medevac, and do you mind being back?"

"I started having chest pain during combat assaults. They want me to go to Landstuhl for a stress test. I don't mind coming back. Flying a helicopter is riding a bike. Everything comes right back."

This CWO was the heat. Vietnam vet, enjoying retirement, and now back to war in his 50s. The army must really have been short on helicopter pilots to bring back retirees. It was phenomenal to have such experience in the cockpit. War was for a young body.

Our patient loads reflected this as older Guard and Reserve members showed up on the manifest. I would bet that this was the oldest military ever sent overseas by the United States. It might be the oldest army ever to fight. The aged human body cannot take the beating of desert combat like a nineteen-year-old.

When we landed at Ramstein, there were two hours remaining on our twenty-four hour duty day. The CMC ordered us to restock our kits right after we finished cleaning up the dirty needles, blood, vomit, and gallons of garbage that had been created from the mission. We normally restocked the next day, but there was a shortage of crews and we were needed back in BRAVO alert. There were more days when there was no legal crew to fly urgent missions, a direct result of sending crews home early.

"Mission Accomplished."

I was tired and didn't want to restock. I wanted bed. I wanted a drink. I remembered the last time I restocked after a mission and loaded the wrong needles in our IV kits.

Tom was MCD, and I started arguing with him that twenty-two hours was a long enough day. Tom felt obligated to get back into BRAVO. We erupted into a heated argument on the ramp. The yelling took place in front of our enlisted medics and the ground support troops. Everyone stared quietly as we yelled. I set a record for using the word fuck. Jaws dropped as enlisted watched in shock at the verbal slugfest.

It wasn't personal. It was fatigue from months of military bullshit and caring for hundreds of wounded. It was a nonproductive argument and the only time I was mad at Tom. After the fight, we ended up calling it a day and went to bed. The kits could wait.

The next day, I realized we were quarrelling because of exhaustion. I was embarrassed for both of us. We had lost our heads and professionalism. Tom and I were cool toward each other for a few days and avoided time off together. The next mission erased the dispute.

# June 24, 2003

Crew Hansen is alerted for an urgent mission. Three urgent and seven priority patients that needed evacuated. Our C-141 fleet was falling apart, and none of the dedicated air evac planes on the ramp were flyable. They put us on a pristine C-17. The C-17 was the plane we'd trained on for the last two years. The war had an ongoing shortage of airlift, and there were not enough aircraft for all the missions. The other drawback was that no funding had been provided for extra litter stanchions. Consequently, we could only carry nine litter patients.

I asked the operations center for extra stanchions. The ops officer explained that there were only nine litter patients, so we didn't need extra stanchions. The crew knew from experience that our patient load would double by the time we landed in the desert. There were no spare stanchions on the base.

We were bused out to the plane to configure. While driving out, I saw a C-17 that has been sitting on the ramp for a few days. I grabbed a crew chief and asked, "Hey chief, that plane over there is hard broke, right?"

"Yeah, that's right. Waiting for parts. It will be grounded another three or four days."

"Great, we need the extra stanchions off that plane for this urgent mission. I already cleared it with Captain Tuttle in the ACC (Airlift Control Center). Don't worry, we'll have those stanchions back in less than twenty-four hours. This mission is a down and back."

The chief looked at me quizzically. He looked at my rank and name tag.

"Okay. If the ACC says it's okay, I'll go get them. But you'll have to sign for them, sir."

"No problem."

I walked onto the massive ramp of the C-17. It was a large tongue sticking out on the tarmac, licking up crew, passengers, and cargo. Tom was directing the configuration and preflight. He asked about the stanchions. I winked and said, "Don't worry. Captain Tuttle is getting them for us." The *M*A*S*H* writers would have been proud.

As I was waiting for the stanchions, I preflighted and helped arrange the medical equipment. I couldn't help but notice the efficiency of the C-17. The lighting was almost blinding. I wouldn't have to wear my headlamp. There was no leaking hydraulic fluid. The floor was clean with no vomit or blood. The temperature within was well maintained and uniform throughout the plane. The C-17 was a generation ahead of the C-141 for patient care. The transport had a new car smell.

A spacious C-17 with litter patients. Aircraft is well lit and better suited for patient care. A lack of litter stanchions limited the amount of patients it could carry.

The crew chief came back with the stanchions and I signed the hand receipt "Capt. Tuttle." He didn't notice and I didn't care, I just wanted to move as many patients as possible.

We launched fifteen minutes early without maintenance issues or gremlins. The flight down was so comfortable that I actually slept four solid hours. It was good, quality sleep and I felt rested. It would be the only sleep we would get in a thirty-three hour period.

In Kuwait, the ramp officer told us we had thirty litter patients and twenty-five ambulatory. I was bumming. We didn't get enough litter stanchions. With our critical patients, we could only carry thirteen litter patients. Four of the litters would be needed to hold the ventilators and critical care equipment. We discussed loading the wounded on the floor and decided against it. There was limited floor space, and another plane was scheduled to land behind us. It was the first time that our crew had to turn back patients and leave them in the desert. I had a personal policy of leaving no one behind. It grated at me. The lack of litter stanchions would continue to plague us for the rest of the deployment. On later flights, crews had no choice but to load our wounded warriors on the floor. This was problematic for patients with Foley catheters and chest tubes—or any other kind of device that requires gravity to flow. The issue with the lack of litter stanchions was not fixed until a complaint was filed with Congressman Adam Smith.

We're flying to Germany with thirty-eight souls. The patients on the plane were primarily Guard and Reserve with noncombat injuries. These patients were support troops and not the hardened combat troops I was used to caring for. I noticed more whining out of this patient load. Some of the patients had medical conditions that I would not consider worth evacing. It was not my decision, and I treated them all the same.

It was disappointing though. I was proud to be in the Reserves. I considered myself a military professional, trained and ready to carry out the assigned mission. Many of these patients did not seem prepared for war. Some of them were overweight or out of shape. I have no statistics to back it up but at least on a few missions, it appeared a disproportionate amount of Guard and Reserve were being flown out of the war zone for frivolous reasons.

I knew some of the front-line combat troops that I had cared for would never leave their comrades for something like "nondescript chronic knee pain."

We delivered the patients safely to Germany. Though it has been a long day, my body felt better after flying on the C-17. The plane's environment was comfortable compared to the austere conditions of the fluid-leaking dehydrator of the C-141.

There was one more mission for the month of June. This flight still haunts me.

# A Mission to Baghdad

*June 28, 2003 Army Sgt. Timothy M. Conneway, 22, of Enterprise, AL Died of wounds suffered June 26 in Baghdad when an explosive device detonated and struck his vehicle. Assigned to the 3rd Battalion, 75th Ranger Regiment, Fort Benning, GA. - U. S. Army Times*

BRAVO alert. Not much was going on. Jeremy Parker and I were passing time watching BBC World News. News flash! There are multiple ambushes and firefights around Baghdad. Several hours later, we were alerted for an urgent mission to that very place. There were seven combat casualties to pick up. By the time we got to the flight line, the number had jumped to fifteen, with three critical patients. With no flyable evac planes, we jumped on a cargo mission. Just as engines started, word was passed that the patient count had again jumped—to thirty.

Flying downrange, I attempted to nap on one of the pallets, but kept waking up, startled and unsure of my surroundings. I decided to get up and inventory combat equipment. I hadn't looked at this stuff since May 1, when major hostilities had ended. I took time to inspect the gas mask and survival vest. I made sure every piece of equipment was in working order. Others on the crew woke and prepared for the combat entry checklist. There was some discussion about whether or not we needed to don all of our equipment. Baghdad International Airport was a secure airfield, and some felt it was overkill to gear up. Tom and I tried to impress upon the crew that the protective equipment was for the flight in and out—not for our time on the ground. Planes were still targeted and shot at in Iraq. A CCATT said, "What does it matter? If we get shot down, there is no chance of surviving a C-141 crash." A fatalistic attitude is a bad state of mind to have on a crew.

I decided to don body armor, helmet, and side arm. I kept the rest close by. Some of the crew elected not to gear up. A few didn't care anymore, and the CCATT team was unaware of the combat entry checklist. The loadmaster switched to red lights before entering Iraqi airspace. It was difficult to see until our eyes adjusted to the dim crimson glow. My crewmates were shadows with faces. The lighting induced a conditioned Pavlovian response—heart and respiratory rates elevated.

I looked out the escape hatch window at the landscape. All exterior lighting was off to conceal the cargo plane within the night sky. A crescent moon was setting. There was enough illumination to silhouette the *Starlifter* and see slivers of landscape. Portions of Iraq were lit while other areas were without power.

I had eyes fixed outside when without warning four flares launched from our defensive system. The interior of the plane flashed hot for just a moment as the flares dropped away from the jet. The light reminded me of flashover training at firefighter recruit academy. I looked back inside. Those without equipment were frantically snapping their Kevlar helmets and body armor in place. I had to smile—the reality of being in a combat zone had sunk in. We had no idea if we were targeted by a SAM or if it was a glitch in the defensive system.

The jet maintained altitude until close to Baghdad. A rapid descent to the airfield minimized exposure. We pitched nose down and held onto the sidewall seats to keep from sliding forward. I was happy that our pilots were former special operations low-level (SOLL) aircrew. They flew a stellar deliberate approach, dropping over eight thousand feet a minute.

Some of the aircrews had no tactical experience and lumbered onto the airfield. The crew that day, active duty out of McGuire AFB, New Jersey, flew aggressively. It was a spiraling roller coaster ride to the desert.

We landed with a jolt and taxied into parking. Cargo was offloaded, and we reconfigured the plane for wounded. We waited . . . and waited. We passed the time looking at our new surroundings and talking with the Security Forces fire team defending our airplane. Looking off in the distance, tracer fire angled out across the sky. There were several flashes on the horizon, followed by fires burning. The fire team said not to worry, that the flashes were most likely confiscated Iraqi munitions being burned.

Finally, an exhausted medic came out from the field hospital. He explained, "We just had several ambushes within the city. The wounded are still coming in. We *need* you guys to wait for a helicopter bringing more. We are overwhelmed and need to get the wounded out."

His appeal confirmed that the flashes were actual ambushes and firefights. As we waited, there were several more flashes and fires. We were on the ground the same night that multiple arson fires were set to initiate ambushes. It was a sophisticated, organized attack in an increasingly lethal guerrilla war.

The medevac helicopter landed, and we assumed our patients would arrive soon. The Humvee driver who came to pick up our CCATTs told us that we had three critical patients on ventilators. One patient was in cardiac arrest with multiple GSWs to the head and chest. Another helicopter was inbound, and we needed to wait for those patients.

The pilots were concerned that dawn was approaching. They wanted to leave before daylight to minimize exposure to ground fire. What could we do? This was where we had to weigh our risks of enemy fire against getting the wounded out. The driver told us not to worry, that C-17s take off all the time in the daylight. We knew that the C-17 was a far more capable aircraft than our aging C-141.

**Dawn at Baghdad International Airport, June 28, 2003**

A thin ribbon of light formed the horizon as dawn colored the sky. The soot from the burning fires created one of the most striking sunrises I have ever witnessed. Patients arrived as daylight illuminated the city. The CCATT doctor reported that the critical in cardiac arrest would not be coming. He was no longer coding, but was too unstable for flight. It was a tough call, but the surgeon believed that the patient could not handle the stress of flight and would certainly die. The soldier died a few hours after we left.

We loaded thirty-eight patients on the plane, the majority of them combat injuries. More medevac choppers landed, but we had to go. Another urgent mission was generated to pick up those wounded. The ambushes continued.

The flight back to Germany was reminiscent of March. Chaos. Stress. No breaks. The worst patient assigned to me was a ranger with a severe wound to the buttocks and thigh. Remember the movie *Forrest Gump* and how Forrest makes light of being wounded in the ass? Seeing an actual wound like that produced no laughter. This was real life, not a movie. The torn and shredded muscle meant difficulty walking, permanent disability, and a changed life.

This ranger was nineteen years old, but looked to be about fifteen. His ranger haircut had grown out a bit and made him look like a teenage punk rocker. He was prone on the litter, facing the two critical patients. His arms dangled over the side.

As I walked by, his left arm reached up and grabbed my calf. He was loaded with morphine and was difficult to understand. He was rambling, "Take care of my buddies . . . *take care of my buddies*, don't worry about me . . . are they going to be *okay?* Are they going to *live?*"

I finally figured out what was going on. The critical patients he was facing were his friends. I had no idea.

When we loaded the patients, we had no time to take into consideration the patients' relationships. He was looking directly at his friends while the CCATTs worked desperately to maintain their lives.

As the flight continued, I got bits and pieces of what happened. The fog of war certainly influenced the telling, and I'm sure I don't have the whole story. This is my best approximation of what happened.

Five Army Rangers were on patrol when a remote control homemade bomb was detonated under them. Hidden Iraqi irregulars then sprayed the soldiers with small-arms fire. One ranger died at the scene, and another died at the field hospital. We got the three survivors. My patient was the only one still conscious.

Each time I walked by the ranger, he reached up and grabbed my leg, asking about his friends. I went over to the CCATT Nurse Brody and asked him how they were doing. He told me, "I got one guy who's shot through the neck and is paralyzed. The other guy has multiple shrapnel wounds and a severe brain injury. These guys are messed up. I hope they killed the fuckers that did this."

I looked at Brody. He was visibly angry. Our CCATT teams treated the hardest patients. The massive injuries were wearing on all of us. The CCATTs felt it the worst.

Critical care nurse preparing medications for severely wounded young soldiers.

Halfway home, I finally caught up on my patients. I couldn't remember their injuries. I sat down to chart on a patient and fell asleep for a moment. Instantly, I was dreaming of wounded and woke with a start.

*Exhausted.*

I looked up to see the prone ranger waving for help. He was in pain. I gave him a touch of morphine. I had to judge how much he had already received. It was easy to over- or under-medicate a patient on these long missions. Lucky for me, I had damn good medics that kept me out of trouble.

Thirty minutes later Amara, one of the newer medics on our crew grabbed me, wide-eyed. "The ranger's not breathing well."

I was too tired to get excited. I looked at him. He was out cold, breathing eight times a minute and drooling. Heart rate was 165 with an oxygen saturation of 65 percent. Too much morphine for the cabin altitude.

Amara administered high-flow oxygen. I slapped his face, but he didn't respond. The oxygen helped, and he stabilized, but was still unresponsive. I didn't want to reverse the narcotic because he'd be in pain again. I sat with him for awhile to make sure he was okay. The thought balloon in my head mocked me. *You're responsible. You gave him too much morphine you dumb shit. His life is in your hands. His life . . . a* human *life. You cannot fail him or his comrades.*

The burden weighed heavy and added to my fatigue. I intently watched the movement of his chest expanding, gasping air from a mask.

He finally woke and motioned to me. I leaned in. Our faces were inches apart. I smelled heated breath that lacked a toothbrush and was dried from opiates. His tongue was chalky white encased by cracked lips. He questioned, "*How...are...my...buddies?*"

"They're alive." Barely.

He vomited. The partially digested MRE stuck to my flight suit and serpentines into the tracks of the cargo floor. I deserved it for overdosing the ranger. The smell of bile kept both of us awake for the remainder of the flight.

I have no memory of the patient offloads—I was on autopilot at that point. Crew rest by midday and disturbing dreams.

\*\*\*

A day later, I spoke with the CCATT team about our patients. My young ranger emphasized one particular patient. In the fog of war, I mixed up the names . . . told him his friend was still alive when actually he had died at the field hospital. I didn't realize the mistake until I debriefed with the CCATT. I felt like shit for this mistake. I hoped this soldier was too drugged to remember.

I felt guilty.

Guilty for leaving wounded behind.

Guilty that we left to protect our own asses and aircraft.

Guilty for not being more alert during the mission.

Guilty for falling asleep in-flight.

Guilt for overmedicating the ranger.

Guilty for mistaking the names of the dead and living.

I drank to try and forget. That didn't work. I tried to run and workout to feel better. That didn't work either.

The stress of caring for these guys. Every mission I flew increased the chances that I was going to make a dangerous mistake. The fatigue added to the risk. Someone was going to die, and I couldn't accept it.

I thought about catching the bus over to Landstuhl Hospital and explaining to the ranger what had happened, and to set the story straight. I never got the chance. We went back into BRAVO alert and readied for the next mission.

The CMC squeezed us on one more mission before the end of June. We were alerted and dragged our bags out to the bus that would take us to the jet. As we were loading, other squadron members were yelling from the BBQ pavilion. A party had just started. Heavy, overloaded coolers of beer were dragged to the pavilion. A respiratory therapist was lighting charcoal. Dark smoke rose from the pavilion and drifted over the bus, inviting us. The medics, nurses, and doctors at the party taunted us to join them. They laughed as we boarded for our next mission. I was the last one on the bus. The bus driver, in a thick German accent and with European body odor, reported factually, "You not going anywhere. I have friend on flight line. He say . . . plane been broken all day. You stay here today."

Before this war, I would not trust the word of a foreign national. I would have thought that the mightiest military in the world would not call unless the jet was flyable. I had learned that the command center was often wrong, that the planes were frequently broken, and that the guys driving the bus were always right.

I ran inside to call CMC. CMC answered the phone with the statement, "It's not our fault. No one told us the plane was broken."

I answered, "The German bus driver told us the plane was broken all day. If the bus driver knows, I think our own command center should know. Now that we are alerted, what are you going to do with us?"

"There's no plane for you to crew. You are released for twelve hours and legal to fly in the morning."

I ran back to the bus, performing calculations in my head. The crew knew I had a mental slide rule that could formulate how long we could drink. The air force regulations state crews cannot imbibe twelve hours prior to the plane taking off.

Rounding the corner to the bus and figuring the earliest time possible we will be airborne and jumped on the bus as the last computation was added.

"We have been released for twelve hours. We are legal for alert at 0715. We can drink till 2230 tonight."

The bus erupted into cheers. Bags were flying assholes to elbows trying to offload so we could join the party.

By the time we changed into civvies, food was on the grill and the beer was flowing. It was worthy, strong, bottled German beer. The CCATT teams had made a mixed Kool-Aid-looking drink that they had named Blue Dawn. I had learned to stay away from mixed drinks in a punch bowl.

The party really spooled up, and the German beer was giving me a buzz. Some people were starting to dance, and I could see one couple walk off.

We had been together four months. Many said we were not part of the real military because of our familiarity with each other and lack of discipline. This was typical in the medical corps. There were no ranks at the party. Enlisted and officers danced and drank together. We were tired of the fucking war and wanted to let go. It was a genuine *M*A*S*H* party.

I started dancing with a sergeant. She was soft to touch and smelled good. I thought about how long it had been since I had touched my wife. I held her a little tighter. We breathed in unison and were acutely aware of each other. I felt the sexual tension. Her hand cradled the nape of my neck. I pressed my hand into the small of her back. The girl was comforting in my arms . . .

Jeremy yelling that we were out of Blue Dawn brought me back to reality.

I broke off the dance. "You'll pay a price for drinking the Blue Dawn Jeremy."

He leaned in to me, reporting, "The chief nurse's car is in the parking lot. Any ideas?"

I was sick of the chief nurse and her lack of support or understanding. I wanted to blow her car up, but I wasn't a combat engineer. "Sgt. Parker, get all the toilet paper you can find. We're going on a mission."

"Ja sächlich, Captain!"

We moved in drunken stealth. We thought we were moving like two trained killers. Partiers watched two drunken reservists who didn't give a damn.

We sneaked to the chief nurse's car and covered it with toilet paper. I wanted to piss on the tires but noticed a dozen people watching. I finished the job by sticking our unofficial squadron patch on the bumper.

Jeremy and I returned to our rooms, too drunk to drink. It was a horrible night of sleep. Hearing Jeremy vomit Blue Dawn every few hours kept me tossing.

We woke to find the room trashed: vomit on the rim of the toilet, a broken margarita glass, clothes strewn about, and empty cardboard toilet paper rolls. The toilet paper adhered to the car.

The chief nurse was offended that someone had violated her car. I was sick of taking care of violated bodies. She was upset over toilet paper. I should've pissed on the tires.

Buildings were searched, and we were implicated because there was no toilet paper in our room. Our crimes were not pursued because of a more wretched offense later in the week.

Someone hung an oversized pink dildo in front of the chief nurse's door with a handwritten sign stating, "What goes around comes around."

**Unofficial squadron patch**

An official investigation was conducted over the dildo. Who would commit such crimes against humanity? Jeremy and I were suspects, but the mission logs confirmed we were airborne when the offense was committed. A respiratory therapist was caught after intense interrogation. Jokes flew regarding how the dildo was connected to her. Was there a fit test like OJ's gloves? She was sent home for her lewd behavior. I wished I'd thought of the vibrator.

# Scorching and Swamped with Patients

July 1, 2003 *US soldiers, the target of increasing attacks by Saddam Fedayeen, Death Squads and other Saddam Fighters, have also had to deal with criminals that were let out of jail by Saddam and the criminality in the capital following the war in Iraq. - Ali Haider*

I was MCD for the flight. The crew had decided to switch crew positions every third mission. Most crews had the senior ranking officer as MCD for the duration of the deployment. Each crew position had its own stress, and the rotation helped sanity. The stress of responsibility wore the MCD. To make it worse, the MCD had all the responsibility but little authority to call the shots. We were micromanaged at every level. The MCD called back to MOTHER (the control center) at Illinois for permission. The chief nurse was dictating how we ran our crews, down to little details like how we took breaks during a flight. It was hard to be an effective leader when you had the responsibility for the lives

147

of your crew and patients but no authority. If anything failed, the MCD was responsible, even if a senior officer (who hadn't flown in years) back in the United States or Germany was giving the order.

We transited to Kuwait with the crew management cell (CMC) that was at Sicily. Sicily was closed. We had busted so many crew duty days that our squadron opened a stage in Kuwait. We would base out of Kuwait and reduce our duty day by ten hours.

That didn't happen that day. We had to fly the round trip from Germany to Kuwait and back. The previous day's flight was scrubbed because of a broken C-141. Yesterday's patients were rolled into our mission. We were asked to wait for several helicopters and a C-130 transiting patients. Time was wasted, and I asked the arriving aircraft to ERO (engine running on-load) the patients directly to the back of our plane. No go. There were concerns about training, and the local Kuwaiti authorities weren't comfortable with two running aircraft so close to each other. As I watched the aircraft approach, I thought about my squadron commander back at McChord lecturing that we would never work with helicopters.

I looked around and realized we were the focal point. Patients from all over the Middle East were flying in to evac on our jet. Helicopters were buzzing back and forth.

A heavy lift CH-47 Chinook helicopter landed close to pick up patients returning to duty. I looked to see if there was anyone on the crew from the Reserve unit out of Ft. Lewis. The twin-rotor helicopter was on the ground for only moments, and then it was airborne again, flying back north into Iraq.

Bob, who was the primary care nurse, confronted me. "Ed, this is dangerous. Too many patients for our crew. Where do we draw the limit on number of bodies we carry? It's risky nursing." Bob was shaking his head.

"I agree, Bob, but if we don't take these patients, they will have to sit here another day. Then the burden is passed to the crew behind us. We have a good crew. I wouldn't do this on every mission, but we can handle it this one time."

**UH-60 Helicopters and C-130 transport aircraft, bringing us patients from all over the Middle East.**

Bob did not argue. My order stood as the crew director. I could tell he wasn't happy. I wasn't happy either, but I didn't like leaving patients behind. My judgment was clouded from the guilt of leaving wounded in Baghdad. Weighing the risks and benefits for the patients was my decision. I knew the crew could handle it. They were that good.

The C-130 arrived with the last of our patients.

Because we couldn't ERO with the helicopters or planes, precious time was lost, threatening our day. Jeremy reported that there was not enough room for all of the patients.

I directed the medics to open as many seats as possible. The ground duty officer and a nurse from the field hospital approached to give me a patient report. I asked how many patients he had.

"However many seats and litters you have available, that's how many patients you have." The duty officer explained the problem.

**Cross loading patients from C-130 turboprop onto our C-141 jet.**

"We packed for home. The war was over and we already shipped staff back to the US. We're a fifty-bed MASF that can hold for four to six hours. We have over a hundred patients. Some have been waiting over twenty-four hours. The least injured patients are in a separate tent with no nursing staff. We're stretched thin at Camp Wolf."

There was room for seventy-eight patients, and that was what was given. With our aircrew and medical crew onboard, there were 110 souls onboard. It was a record.

Fatigue bent memory. The combination of long duty days and the volume of bodies combined into one elongated, nightmarish mission. My flight log book, personal journal, and photographs were a way to arrange the individual missions. When I sorted them in my mind, I was baffled.

A photo jogged the memory of a patient. He was an Australian sound engineer that was wounded during an RPG attack. He worked for NBC. I tried to talk to the patient, but he was so gorked out on morphine that it was hard to have a meaningful conversation. I watched as a critical care nurse injected medicine into his IV. His coworker sat next to me and narrated. He handed me the shrapnel that had struck down his friend.

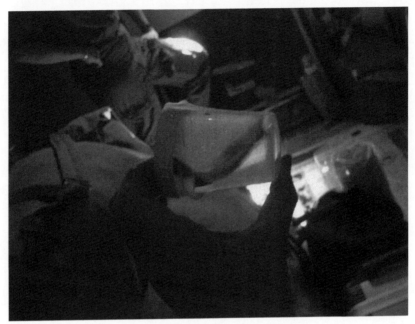

**The metal shrapnel that killed a patient.**

A little piece of metal devastated the human body. It was a large wound in his buttocks and thigh. By the time we landed, I knew so much about this man that it was personal.

At parking, a media circus was waiting. It was immense news when a journalist got wounded or killed. A public affairs officer (PAO) reported that the sound engineer's parents were on the tarmac and that they would like some photos with his family reunited.

With as much tact as I could muster, I pushed back the PAO. "Under no circumstances will any camera or family member walk onto this airplane. Every one of the seventy-eight patients deserves to see their family, not just one person. This will not turn into a media show. Your cameras will have to wait."

There were no arguments and we offloaded without incident. A few days later, the *Stars and Stripes* reported that the Australian, who was only twenty-seven, died of complications to his wounds.

This hit me in the chest like shrapnel. I recognized that though my crew had never lost a patient in-flight, some of our patients had died. It may have been the next day at Landstuhl or weeks or months later back in the States, but some of our patients were dead. I thought about the dead listed by the military. They maintained a very accurate roster of servicemen killed in action (KIAs).

KIAs were reported on the evening news. Great emphasis had been placed on how many had died since President Bush declared major combat over. But what about the ones who died of wounds at later dates? No one was reporting the nineteen-year-old lying in a VA hospital or at Walter Reed who died of horrific wounds long after battle, or the suicides from combat stress. The reason I knew about the death of the sound engineer was his employment at NBC. A GI buried weeks or months after combat was not newsworthy.

# Kuwait in July

The Fourth of July was my favorite holiday. Back home, I would attempt to take that day off. The tradition for friends in the Reserves was a party in downtown Tacoma. We drank during a gluttonous BBQ and watched the air show and fireworks.

On July 4, 2003, we landed in Kuwait and entered the new stage. I assumed we were to lodge in the tent city with the rest of the military stationed at the international airport. For reasons I cannot begin to answer, we were sent downtown to the Kuwaiti Sheraton hotel.

We changed into civvies for downtown. Though Kuwait was liberated in 1991, there were plenty of people that hated Americans. Departing the airport, I noticed that our jet was easily seen from the freeway. The plane was an open target for someone with an RPG or machine gun. We drove past a Kuwaiti armored vehicle with a fifty-caliber gun mounted in the top turret. The MP escort informed us that the Humvee was posted after terrorists were caught setting up a machine gun within range of our parking spot. The ride was uneventful, but our crew was an inviting soft target. We arrived at the hotel and were swarmed by doormen and bagboys.

This was a hotel for the elite. It was plush and opulent. Heads of state transited here. It was also burned out and looted by the Iraqis in the first Gulf War. The downside of the hotel was that there was no booze and we were restricted to the property. The hotel was superior to tent city and no one complained. It was air force living.

# July 7, 2003

*The Bush administration concedes that evidence that Iraq was pursuing a nuclear weapons program by seeking to buy uranium from Africa, cited in January State of the Union address and elsewhere, was unsubstantiated and should not have been included in speech. Over the summer, Tony Blair faces even stronger criticism than his American counterpart concerning flawed intelligence.*

*At Baghdad University in Baghdad, a US soldier was standing in line with other Iraqis waiting to buy a soda when a Saddam fighter dressed in civilian clothes came up behind him and shot him in the head. The soldier reportedly was part of civil assistance group that had been in Iraq helping with food, clean water, and other programs to help the nation that has been decimated under the years of Saddam's regime.*

*-CNN*

The BBC reported our mission. A GI had been shot in the back of the head at Baghdad University, execution-style at close range. Annie Thomas's CCATT team was alerted to take care of the critical patient.

We were out to the plane and sweating weight off, readied for our critical patient. Annie drove to the field hospital to assess. We prepared for a big load of bodies. Annie was back in an hour. She asked us to offload her critical care equipment. Her patient had died. I could only stop for a moment to think about the GI that had lost his life. What had he died for? Hundreds were dying before they reached us. I took an instant and internally mourned the loss of a person I'd never met.

Back to work to care for sixty-eight patients.

We loaded with ease and efficiency. Our crew was seasoned, and we prided ourselves on speed. We had a running bet with the ground troops that they would never wait when it came to loading wounded. Early in the war, we would lose the bet and I would smuggle in a case of beer to pay the debt. We had not lost a bet in months, but I still brought the ground crews beer.

Booze was off-limits in the desert. But I didn't care. Camp Wolf was also staffed by the 47th Combat Support Hospital out of Fort Lewis. These were the same people that my wife worked with at her civilian job at Madigan ER. When I could, I brought a case of beer to ease austere army living.

As the cargo doors were closing, one of the nurses sprinted up with a patient bracelet. She had been weaving these bracelets by hand out of parachute cord for the soldiers with combat wounds. She wrapped it around my wrist and said, "Thank you. You have the best crew in your squadron. Your crew never let us down."

The plane taxied out, and I prepared myself for the worst part of the mission: the takeoff. Once the plane was lined up on the runway, we left our patients' sides seat-belted in. On rare occasions, when a patient was too critical to leave, the nurse would strap to the patient's litter and stand for takeoff. That day we sat and rode out the takeoff and climb-out till we were above potential threats. During that time, the nurses and medics were powerless. My mind wandered, and I thought about things that could go wrong. Would someone shoot at us? Would the plane hold up to the stresses of the desert? Would all of my patients still be alive once I was cleared to walk around? I looked down at the rows of bodies and had no way of telling how they were doing. I thought of this during the takeoff. I realize how helpless I was and how little control I had over the events that occurred around me and influenced my life. I was the most fearful during takeoff. If I could have gotten out of my seat and buried myself in patient care, I wouldn't have dwelled.

Loading patients up the ramp of the C-141.

Once the plane was at a safe altitude, we immediately noticed a problem with pressurization. At first no one was worried, because it had happened before. We had lost a rubber seal earlier from a side escape hatch and filled in the gap with wet paper towels.

Our ears were popping, and the flight engineer noticed that the pressure door had developed a bulge. The corner lock had also pulled tight from the pressure. The flight engineer advised us to stay seat-belted as much as possible and not to let anyone near the ramp without a restraint harness on. My interphone plug-in was at the back of the jet. I was seated closest to the pressure door.

During the course of the flight, our cabin altitude fluctuated as one of the pressurization packs died. I was able to monitor this with the altimeter on my wristwatch. The rapid change in pressure was dangerous for patients. As the cabin rose in altitude, the existing pressure decreased. This lack of pressure could play havoc on a chest tube or stop a drip IV from flowing. Patients with oxygenation problems had to be closely watched.

The cabin altitude rapidly jumped from 6,800 feet to twelve thousand feet. The flight engineer caught this before the warning horn could sound. The system was no longer functioning properly, and the engineer manually controlled the pressure for the duration of the flight. The pilots minimized their time in the cargo hold because of the bulging pressure door. They stayed locked up on the flight deck. We landed, and I was anxious from the pressure problems. There was a knot in my stomach.

My altimeter watch was broken from the rapid pressure changes.

# Back to the States

## July 9, 2003

We loaded for a mission to America. The original plan was for the downrange crews to fly strictly to the desert. There was supposed to be dedicated medevac crews in Germany to evac wounded to the States. Our CO and chief nurse decided it would be good for morale if everyone flew some combat missions. They thought morale would improve if all drew hostile fire pay and tax-free money.

The problem with the plan was that the dedicated stateside crews had no combat equipment to fly into the war zone. They didn't have any survival vests, desert uniforms, or Kevlar. Some had no weapons. Our supply sergeant started collecting our combat gear to loan to the stateside crews.

The plan was a nightmare. Weapons and survival vests were lost. I worked so hard to acquire survival equipment for my crew that we refused to give up our gear. My Berretta was lost in the shuffle and I never saw it again. I was issued someone else's gun and was told not to worry. To this day, I'm not sure all the weapons and survival gear were ever accounted for.

When we arrived stateside, I was anxious to see how the war was portrayed on American TV. Sick of the biased BBC and Kuwaiti broadcast reports. I flipped through the US channels and couldn't find news on the war. The top story of the day was about a baseball team mascot shaped like a giant sausage being knocked over with a baseball bat by Pittsburgh Pirate Randall Simon. Every channel was engrossed in the life-size sausage being toppled over. The scene was replayed over and over.

Finally, toward the end of the world news, there was a twenty-second clip mentioning a GI killed in an ambush. The story was an afterthought of the day's news, and certainly not as important as an enormous meat casing beaten by a Pirate. I was disgusted. Who knew or cared about the patients we were evacing? I turned off the TV and banged out an e-mail home.

### Ambush

Early in the war, my patients were angry at the ambushes. They came onto the plane visibly upset at being jumped and not being able to return fire. Later, during the peak of the ground war, my wounded GIs had colorful stories of combat and being able to engage the enemy. There was a sense of gratitude at being able to fight back.

The war had returned to hit-and-run tactics. The deposed Iraqis knew they could not win a large-scale battle, so they whittled us down one soldier at a time. Those tactics were having a disturbing effect on my patients.

They didn't board the plane discussing battles fought. They no longer released their emotions—they didn't have the energy for it. The wounded patients were worn down and exhausted. They stared into space and said little. Even a meal of pizza and fresh-baked cookies did not elicit the joyful responses we had at Easter.

The heat had weathered the troops. I used to be able to tell the combat injured from noncombat injuries just by facial expressions. The high temperatures and long deployment had left everyone with the same vacant look. I had to read their charts to distinguish the injuries.

One patient's chart noted that he had multiple shrapnel injuries and bilateral ruptured eardrums. When I approached him, he was sitting, lost in thought. He didn't look wounded except for some scratches on his face. I asked him about his injuries to make sure I had the correct medical record. He lifted up his shirt and pant legs to show the scars. There were peppered marks all over his body from RPG shrapnel and shards of his Humvee.

The soldier had been on mounted patrol in Baghdad. They had been driving down a street when he noticed the car traffic was increasing around their vehicle. The traffic began to slow, and he started to worry. He looked for a way to turn around, but could not find a spot in the narrow city streets. The traffic came to a standstill, and several children appeared. They approached the convoy and asked for candy. The soldier felt fear. It was a setup, and there was nothing he could do to stop it. They were stopped in traffic, and children were attempting to distract him. He swiveled his head, probing for a gunner on a rooftop or in a window. His comrades pointed their M-16 rifles out, searching for the ambush. His words were laced in fear.

"I knew we were dead. I unholstered my pistol and released the safety. I pointed the weapon directly at the children and yelled at them to leave now. The children would not move. Then an RPG blasted our Humvee. I never saw the gunner or the rocket. I was thrown from the vehicle. My flak vest and helmet were destroyed. My clothing was shredded . . . I was practically naked. Blood was running from my ears, and I had small bleeding holes all over. My buddies helped me to a corner of a building. We cowered, trying to make ourselves small. I was dazed and felt exposed without my nine mil. I have no idea what happened to it. We looked down the road—the street was deserted. The traffic jam and children were gone." Help arrived later to get them safely to base camp.

As I listened to his story, it struck me that this was not a random act of violence. It was a well-coordinated attack involving children, cars, spotters, and a shooter. It was painfully clear that we shouldn't underestimate the Iraqis that opposed us: they were smart, harmonized in their approach, and were successfully using guerrilla tactics.

Telling the story brought back this soldier's fear. He saw the elephant. I was afraid just listening to him. I admired his courage for being able to patrol, knowing each day that he could be ambushed. He said it was not courage; he was scared on every patrol. I think that is true courage—to know the risks, to be scared, and still perform your job.

Like many of my wounded, the soldier vigorously expressed how lucky he was to be alive. Its a central moment in this GI's life. He told me he had twelve years in and had previously planned a full twenty-year career. At that moment on the plane, the soldier had no idea what he was going to do. He didn't know if he was going to stay in the military, but it didn't matter. He was alive—that was enough for now.

Captain Ed 'RIV' Hrivnak

Instructor Flight Nurse

Coming home soon

# Rumors of Home

The rumors that we might be shipping home were coming true. Replacement medevac crews arrived in Germany. A new CMC had reported to replace our command group. Jennifer was discharged from active duty. She immediately hopped on a military transport and flew to Germany, hoping to see me.

When I returned from the US, we were given seventy-two hours off. It was the first time in Germany that we had more than twenty-four hours off. Precious time off was granted in hours, not days or weeks.

It was overwhelming to see Jennifer. She was okay. I was more worried about her deployment than my own. She lived in the desert and was exposed to more subjective risks.

For the first time since being activated, I had three days to escape and not report to command. We immediately rented a BMW convertible and left the country, traveling to Luxemburg, Belgium, and back through Bitburg, Germany. We stayed at an undersized hotel that survived the Battle of the Bulge at Bastogne and toured European battlefields. I was awed at the carnage during the World Wars. I thought about the sacrifices of today. Were there going to be any memorials for the liberators of Baghdad?

Three days off were refreshing with Jennifer, except for sleep. I woke in the middle of the night staring at the ceiling, not sure why. Not sure how to get back to sleep. I found myself walking the empty streets of Bastogne before dawn.

I returned to duty, and Jennifer stayed with friends stationed in Germany.

Two more blurred missions. One night while on alert, Jimmy Natio had a DVD for us to watch. It was *Tears of the Sun* with Bruce Willis. No one could enjoy it. War movies were no longer entertainment. They were reminders of reality.

Jimmy was back with us from Sicily and still working German ground support. Not only did he ready planes for missions, he had to load and unload the patients that transited Germany every day. Sometimes this was as many as six aircraft in a shift. Loading and unloading human cargo had become Jimmy's daily routine.

During one of the slow parts in the movie, Jimmy stated, "I'm tired of the bodies. It's depressing."

No one said anything. No eye contact. We were weary from broken bodies, but it wasn't something we discussed. After a long awkward silence, I said, "I'm tired too, Jimmy."

Dead quiet.

The movie continued with graphic battles and Hollywood explosions. No one noticed. . . lost in our own thoughts.

I thought about the wounded. Each crew kept track of how many patients we evacuated. We never counted the days working ground support. Loading a plane involved only a few minutes of contact with each patient. I hadn't considered that we were actually exposed to thousands of casualties while working the ramp. That kind of contact wore on the strongest medic, nurse, or doctor.

I attempted to capture the injured faces that swirled in my head from the last few tangled missions. Unable to sleep, another e-mail home was better than staring at the ceiling.

## Faces of War

The Humvee is like the Pinto of the 1970s: it burns quickly when hit by a rocket. One GI told me he saw his Humvee burn down in less than three minutes. You can't get out of the vehicle fast enough if you're hit.

I was transporting a medical officer who was struck in such a situation. He was hauling medical supplies to Iraqi civilian hospitals when they were ambushed by an RPG. He was burned on most of his upper body and face. The tops of ears were burned off. His arms and hands were covered in heavy bandages, and ointment covered his red, peeling face. I sat and talked with him as we waited for an ambulance.

The officer was prior enlisted, married, and had three children. He decided to become a medical officer to provide better for his family and to get out of the field. He told his family not to worry about him when he went overseas because he would be serving in the rear with medical logistics. He would not be fighting on the front lines. (Where were the front lines in Iraq?)

He was not concerned about his burns, but he was worried about what his children were thinking. He said, "I talked to them on the phone yesterday. They didn't understand why I was burned. I promised them I was going to be okay—that I would be safe. The kids don't get it, and I'm not sure how to explain it to them."

I stared at his face and burns the whole time he was talking. His face was an expressionless mask. I couldn't tell if he was tired like the rest of the patients or if the burns were causing his unvaried, masklike appearance. The tone of his voice when speaking of his children was his only signal of emotion.

On this same flight stateside, I had a Green Beret and premature baby twins. The mother was playing with one of the babies. The Special Forces (SF) soldier was talking with two of his comrades. His face was that of a hardened warrior. The baby's face was innocent and beautiful. The child smiled at its mom. The soldier never smiled. The baby had a whole lifetime to look forward to. The SF soldier was missing his hand and part of his forearm. His future: dark.

I was frozen in place as I took in the juxtaposition of baby and soldier. The mother breast-fed the baby. The soldier had to have help with his meal because he couldn't open a bag of potato chips with only one hand. There was such a stark contrast between the two. The newborn had no idea what war was. The baby's future had endless possibilities. The career soldier wanted to stay with the SF team, but didn't think he could remain in the army with only one hand.

Those faces of war are what I remembered most vividly from that hell. I had tried to describe them, I even had photographs of some, but I wasn't sure that either medium offered a clear picture of how war changed a person's face. I wasn't sure I had succeeded in conveying that over the last five months of writing my journal and e-mails.

If you're ever given the chance, visit the Korean War Memorial in Washington, DC. The faces of the statues reminded me very much of the wounded for whom I had cared. Whoever sculpted those faces captured perfectly the effect of war on the people who fought it.

- Ed Hrivnak, short timer

**Korean War Memorial, Washington, DC**

On our last stage to Kuwait, Jeremy, Tom, and I smuggled in a load of booze. We paid off the hotel manager with two cases of wine for the service and for ensuring our security. Our last act in Kuwait was getting drunk. Fuck General Order Number One. In between beers, we made up a David Letterman-style Top Ten List of our experiences in this deployed composite squadron.

**Top Ten Reasons you know you're trapped in the 491st Expeditionary Aeromedical Evacuation Squadron (EAES)**

10. You avoid Mildenhall and Ramstein at all costs.
9. You wake up and have no idea where you are.
8. You are on alert, but still have to walk to the chow hall to eat.
7. Your 24-hour mission, with body armor, Kevlar, and a tail swap in 114-degree Middle East heat is "just like a ten-hour shift in a hospital."
6. No matter how long the mission was, or how many wounded you crammed into the plane, or how late you landed at Ramstein, you still have to report for duty at 0645 the next morning (even if there is no bus to pick you up).
5. Don't talk to the new guy on your crew; he'll be reassigned by the next mission.
4. You have no idea where your weapon is.
3. The crew management cell has no idea where you are going, the plane is broken, and there is no front-end crew, but you have just been alerted.
2. Aircrews share rooms or sleep at MWR (for proper crew rest). CMC and command personnel have private suites.
1. Your ass hurts.

**Top Ten Things That are Heard at the 491 EAES**

10. From CMC, "It's not our fault, AMCC screwed up." Or, "It's not our fault, TACC screwed up." Or, "It's not our fault."
9. "There will be no sleeping on the plane."
8. "The beatings will continue until morale improves."
7. "You have no idea how rough it is at Rota. We have three missions a week and only sixty-five people to cover the missions."
6. "We don't support TDY people here."
5. "I don't care if you are on active duty. We don't support reservists."
4. "Quit drinking so much. Try taking up learning a new language instead."

3. From the intel officer, "I wouldn't fly into Baghdad."
2. "Is the chief nurse in command or is it our squadron commander? . . . (long pause) . . . who is our squadron commander?
1. Two words: "Plane's broke."

**And for those of you that went through the stage at Mildenhall and saw the poster on the wall: "How about a nice cup of shut the fuck up!"**

Since it was our last stay in Kuwait, I decided to walk the streets and shop. We were human targets and restricted to the hotel. No one cared about rules anymore. I was more worried about the army and marines finding out how the air force was living. I could see a war breaking out between the services if they found out how we fought the war from a hotel.

I bought some gold for Jennifer and a few things for my mom. Walking the streets of Kuwait City made me thankful to live in the United States. The city is blistering, sandy, grimy, and littered with trash. And it has that Middle Eastern smell. One of our docs tried to rent a car and asked the travel agent where the good places are to visit in Kuwait. She answered, "There are no good places to visit in Kuwait."

# Last Mission

July 25, 2003 *US combat deaths in Iraq reach 147,*
*the same number of soldiers who died from hostile fire in the*
*first Gulf War; 32 of those deaths occurred after May 1,*
*the officially declared end of combat. Saddam*
*Hussein's sons, Uday and Qusay Hussein, die*
*in a firefight in a Mosul palace -CNN*

The phone barked and we're alerted for our final flight. Jeremy popped in music to motivate us. He led in with the "Imperial March" from *Star Wars* and followed up with "It's Nice to Go Trav'ling" by Sinatra. I had hoped our last mission would be a milk run. Murphy's Law thrives at war. Instead, we were tasked with an urgent mission out of Camp Wolf with fifty-eight patients, earning our drinks for the eight-hour flight back to Germany.

One patient had significant wounds, but his wounds were not what concerned me. He had been a gunner manning a grenade launcher in the top turret of an armored Humvee. They had driven over a remote-controlled detonated bomb. He said, "The blast covered me with shrapnel, but I didn't think I was seriously injured. The Hummer kept rolling. I couldn't figure out why the driver wasn't stopping. I dropped down the turret to see he's dead. Pushed aside what was left to stomp the brakes. He was my friend."

He, like many, was not concerned about his injuries. The thoughts of the dead and wounded comrades caused the most suffering.

The patient that required the majority of physical attention was a young soldier from the 101st Airborne Division. He was on the strike team that killed Saddam Hussein's sons. He had a gunshot wound to the chest, two chest tubes, and was coughing up blood.

Coughing up blood is not like what you see in the old war movies. It is not a slight, single cough followed by a little trickle of bright red, ketchuppy-looking stuff. (In the movies, the little trickle of ketchup is always neatly placed at the corner of the mouth.) The real blood is dark, bluish red, and it doesn't trickle; it congeals in the lungs and is painfully coughed up like a piece of bubble gum that's down the wrong pipe. The patient has to cough violently to expel the glob.

I tried to keep the soldier sedated until we landed, though I wasn't completely successful. At times during the flight, we talked about combat. He said, "I thought we had them. I was walking back to my Humvee, fairly certain that the battle was over. I was casually standing there when someone from outside the building shot me in the back."

This statement was significant. I'd caught the European news just before the mission. The commentator was upset that overwhelming force was used to kill Saddam's sons, Uday and Qusay Hussein. He wanted to know why the US could not wait to negotiate surrender. Typical of the media, they only had a small piece of what actually happened. The reporter never mentioned that there were loyalists outside the building shooting the Americans from behind. What was reported in the news was only a small slice of the complete story.

I looked at his wound. It was unique. He was adjusting desert goggles with his hands overhead when a sniper shot his right quarter. The projectile entered under his right armpit, missing the body armor. It exited out the chest, striking the front ceramic armor plate. The 7.62 millimeter bullet still had plenty of energy, ricocheted off the plate, and entered the left side of his chest wall. The tumbling missile then exited out the left flank, shattering ribs and taking the air from his lungs with it. Four holes and bilateral collapsed lungs from one bullet. A skilled sniper shot against an armored body. It was not the first time I had seen an armpit wound. The Iraqis had figured out the weaknesses in our armor and our military.

When we landed in Germany, the GI was the last patient off the plane. I held on to his chest drainage units and talked as he was carried him to the ambus. Then I realized that not only was he the last patient off the plane, but he was my last patient for this deployment. The realization and emotion of the moment caught me off guard. I tried to maintain composure as we lifted him into the bus. I got a thumbs-up and a thank-you from the GI. That was all I needed. I knew I had made a difference in the war. I turned away from him to hide wet eyes.

I walked back to the plane and worked on cleaning the disorder. While packing, I thought back through the last five months. I'd aged since peeled from civilian life in February. Volumes of experience occurred in a compressed time period.

I was only on the flight schedule for a hundred and fifteen days. In that time, the crew I served with flew fifty-four sorties and completed eighteen missions. We evacuated nearly eight hundred patients. Our squadron numbers are even more staggering. The 491 Expeditionary Aeromedical Evacuation Squadron existed for half a year. In that squat period, the air force aeromedical system transported more than ten thousand patients, most of them by us. Even though many were noncombat casualties, it was a staggering workload.

Ten thousand patients. The day the Twin Towers came down, I wondered what it would be like to evacuate ten thousand patients. I thought it would take everyone in airevac to move that many bodies. We moved seven thousand patients from the desert to Germany. Three thousand of those patients were then transported to the States. It never occurred to me that I would be a part of a squadron that would move that many souls. It was an astonishing feat for a relatively small number of people.

Though I along with the flight crews bitched about our command staff and CMC, I should give due credit. Somehow this composite squadron from ten different bases pulled it together and accomplished an incredible feat. We stood up a squadron with very little support, almost no funding, and flying on forty year old planes that the air force was ready to scrap. We were strangers at the beginning of the war and had to learn mass casualty evacuation. Even with extensive maintenance problems and extremely long duty days, very few patients died in flight. American military medicine achieved the highest survival rate in the history of combat. Although worn-out, we had reason to be proud of our actions.

When I reflect on this, I recognized that I excelled as a nurse but failed as an officer. I was so concerned about the safety of my crew and patients that I failed to see the big picture. Consequently, I did not support the decisions of the officers above me. The command staff and CMC had to make difficult decisions to keep the mission moving forward. Sometimes our safety had to be compromised. The excessively long missions and lack of proper equipment such as walk-around oxygen bottles and litter stanchions were a result of overall poor logistical planning, for an extended war that was never suppose to happen. Our command staff gambled with what they had and won. Not a single evac plane or crew was lost to accident or combat.

We were now human cargo waiting for a ride back to Washington State. There was a rush to deploy, but there seemed to be no hurry to get us home. We hoped to be home within the next week.

I wasn't sure how to feel about coming home. The war wasn't over. It was far from over. Many of us would have to come back in the winter to relieve the new guys that replaced us. No one knew what the future would bring, but I feared I would not be skiing at Crystal Mountain come winter . . .

# Going Home

## July 27, 2003

After our last mission, there was no preparation for home. The command staff and the rest of the supporting command element had left. They essentially abandoned us in Germany to find our own way home.

I remembered a crusty old navy master diver telling me the first rule of leadership: "Take care of your people, and they will take care of you." Our squadron was disbanded, and a new unit, the 791st EAES was organized in Germany. We missed if there was a ceremony or party to mark the event.

There was no plan, and I didn't give a shit. Replacements arrived and took the missions. I could care less about passing on words of wisdom to the new crews. I avoided them, not even making eye contact. It wasn't my war anymore, and no one cared about us. It was a week before we had an idea of how to get home.

I grabbed Jennifer and took the rented BMW, leaving for Switzerland. We escaped the air force for five days. Jennifer and I had a fantastic time together, exploring the mountains of Garmich, Austria, and Switzerland. We spent a day at the naked

Roman baths at Badin-Badin and managed to visit an old climbing friend and veteran, Rick Barnes, in Stuttgart.

My wife was a gem. She did her best to help me forget. The days were great. The nights were difficult. One night I woke in a cold sweat. I stumbled from bed and stood on the hotel balcony with a moonlit view of the Igier Mountain. Defeated, I dressed and walked the deserted predawn streets of Interlaken. My thoughts were confused, and I couldn't make sense of why I was awake.

It was a rewarding time off together, but I was exhausted from the restless sleep.

Returning to Ramstein, plans were made for home that changed daily. The problem was that the active duty would not take ownership of us and neither would the Reserves. The active duty instructed us to take the rotator home. The rotator is a civilian contracted airliner that transits Frankfurt, Germany, to Baltimore twice a week. There were thirty-five of us, and the plane only had room for ten of us at a time. It would take two weeks for all of us to get home.

Our home unit wanted to send a plane to come get us, but higher command did not approve the mission because we were owned by the active duty. Catch-22.

While details were worked, Tom, Jeremy, Brian, and I volunteered to build the two pallets of cargo that held our personal luggage. We spent the day drinking beer and building pallets on the German flight line. Raising bottles, we toasted medevac jets as they roared off to Iraq.

"Cheers replacements!"

"Good luck in Iraq!"

"Prost!"

We were motivated to build the pallets because there were thirty-nine cases of German beer and wine to smuggle. Each precious crate of German spirits was protected by our own baggage. After the work was done, we continued to drink, playing basketball on a makeshift hoop. It was now pouring down rain and one of the youthful, good-looking medics join us. She was wearing a white T-shirt, and it was quickly wetted and pressed against her firm, uplifting breasts. She might as well have taken her shirt off. We stared at her, making comments under our breath . . . the dirty old men that we are. She acted oblivious to our drunkenness and our undressing her with aged eyes. We were ready for home.

# July 31, 2003

Loaded up on a bus and headed to Frankfurt, looking for home. Jennifer joined the gaggle. At Frankfurt, we did not have the proper paperwork and had to sit standby, flying home two-to-three at a time. We had to break the beer pallets down. This was a crisis. This was crossing the line.

I was told that Jennifer was restricted from any military aircraft. Spouses can fly space available on military aircraft. This perk only applied to spouses of the active duty. Activated reservists were not given the same consideration.

This infuriated me. Once again, the two-tiered system for how reservists recalled to active duty were treated. I was yelling in the passenger terminal: "Get someone else to fight your damn war next time!" Jennifer purchased a two thousand dollar plane ticket home because we were second-class citizens in the eyes of the military.

I had had enough with the bullshit of waiting. I considered the jump orders that were issued at the beginning of the war. I took my orders to the ticket counter and asked the sergeant working the desk if these orders were valid. He said, "Certainly. Those orders are good worldwide."

"I've got jump orders for thirty-five people and would like to space block room on the next plane flying to McChord."

We were chalked on the next flight out on August 1.

The dilemma was that I didn't have jump orders for everyone. We had non-flyers in the group. I gathered everyone together and explained that they should hand me some kind of official-looking paper with their name on it. I then stacked the thirty-five sheets of paper and turned them in with authentic jump orders on top.

When I cleared for processing, the clerk looked at the first ten or so orders, saw they were okay, and blocked the flight.

We waited for boarding time on two C-17s. An aerial port troop reported that one plane was broken and he could only get ten home on the first transport.

I talked to Mary, the pilot in command of our plane. Mary was from Washington and knew most of us. I told her of our plight, and she promised to get us home.

Mary ordered the loadmasters to consolidate the cargo to create more space. She did not have room for all. There was a flight later in the day to get the rest of the gaggle home. We split up based on first in, first out.

The commanding general for the Reserve wing wanted us all together so he could puff his chest while the media filmed the homecoming. We had instructions to fly as one horde. We didn't care. We just wanted to get home.

We crossed the Atlantic to Pope AFB in North Carolina to drop off cargo and troops that had been deployed for nine months. The security police searched with dogs for drugs and war souvenirs. Some returning troops had been caught trying to bring back captured Iraqi weapons. Our plane came up clean. The dogs didn't care about the thirty-nine cases of beer and wine.

We were finally in the US. No excitement. We were not home, and the plane could still break. After refueling, we climbed to the stratosphere for the final five-hour leg home. The transport had plenty of room with most of the cargo and troops gone. We stretched out bags and sought sleep with little success. The anticipation was building.

We entered Washington airspace, and the Cascade Mountain Range welcomed us with mountains and snow. Mount Rainier materialized, announcing that we were close to home.

The plane touched down, holding subdued emotion released with some clapping and a few cheers. We parked in front of the passenger terminal and could see families waiting.

The engines shut down. Families briskly walked to the plane. I don't recall being excited or relieved being home. I was too exhausted. It didn't feel like the homecoming after the first Gulf War. The war was not over, we were still on active duty, and there was a real threat that we would go back.

It was tremendous to see my family and mom. She had the same stressed look she had had when I returned from Desert Storm in 1991. Her twin sons in two wars, and her daughter-in-law in one. She said, "You guys have done your part for your country— let someone else do it now."

There was a homecoming party at the wing bar, *Hangar 13*. Few stayed long. We were somnolent and wanted beds.

\*\*\*

Returning crews were granted two weeks off, so Jennifer and I disappeared by floatplane and helicopter to Alaska and Canada. Isolated in the Canadian frontier on Tagish Lake, Jennifer and I were forced to talk to each other. I found it difficult to confide in her and tell her the fears and guilt I had from the deployment. We struggled to re-learn our marriage. The remote setting of Brookland cabins, with an abundance of fishing and hiking helped me sleep.

The last part of our vacation was spent at Neah Bay, Washington. This was the home of the Makah Nation and Jeremy Parker. Jeremy asked Tom and me to attend his homecoming party. It was a tradition dating back to World War I. Any time a Makah warrior left for a foreign battle, a going away and homecoming ritual was performed. Since its inception, every soldier that put on the American uniform returned home safely.

The Makahs danced and sang to the beat of handmade drums. Traditional jewelry sparkled in sunlight. They presented homecoming gifts to Jennifer, Tom, and me. We were introduced as honorary members of Jeremy's family.

Tom and I wore dress uniforms adorned with accruements of past conflicts and humanitarian service. Jeremy stood tall with shoulders squared, his sergeant stripes blazing white. We presented the Parker family the service medals Jeremy had earned overseas. Tom and I also handed Jeremy a life membership to the VFW. He had earned his status as a Veteran of a Foreign War. It was a unique mix of ancient Indian culture and modern military pomp. Our stay at the extreme northwest corner of Washington State was healing.

# Aftermath

## Mid-August 2003

After two weeks' leave, I reported for duty. Garrison life. Office work. Paper work.

I had no motivation. We had a mountain of training to accomplish. Training had been waived for the war. We were no longer qualified to do our jobs.

The group had to take classes on chemical warfare training, even though we could don a gas mask in seconds after living with one for months. It was typical stateside crap that endured. I didn't want to deal with it. We had inspections and exercises to prepare for. Who cared about an inspection after war?

Crews were warned to prepare to redeploy in November. Some of us would have to go back to fill the manpower shortages overseas.

This really pissed me off. We had people in our squadron that had not deployed yet. Some of them had been promoted while we were gone. Morale in the unit was low and split between those who had gone and those who had remained behind. This was another penalty from the decision to break up the stateside units at the beginning of the war.

Jennifer's group was deployed for six weeks, and they were released when they returned home. My group had been activated and deployed from the squadron the longest and they wanted to ship us back. The burden was not distributed evenly.

There was no long-term strategic plan. We were playing crisis management, throwing bodies wherever there was a fire. No one anticipated or planned for a long, protracted war involving thousands of dead and wounded.

I'd come home from work, frustrated and angry. Being a dumbass, I took my frustrations out on Jennifer.

She tried to be understanding. But I was too much of an asshole. I would explode in fits of rage and yell. I would howl over stuff that neither one of us had control over. I was stupid.

There was more to my behavior than just yelling and anger. I was still losing sleep. Terror would wake me.

Nightmares with night sweats involved all my experiences in nursing and field medicine. In one particularly vivid dream, I'd been shot and the medics were wheeling me to an ambulance. We passed by a large bus, and I stepped out of my body and got in the bus. Inside the bus was every patient that I had ever cared for that died at my hands or died later of their injuries. There were also the dead I had found when volunteering with Mountain Rescue. The deceased were sitting nonchalantly and welcomed me to the group. I stared at their wounds and pasty death masks. They welcomed me as a friend. I was on the wrong bus and yelled for the medics to come back. Looking out the window, the medics were performing CPR on my lifeless body. Blood was oozing from bullet wounds each time they compressed my chest wall. I woke with a start, and my heart was pounding. It was not just dreams that frightened me.

I was startled easily. Loud noises would make me jump. I could not sleep in the car. If I did doze off, the slightest tapping of the brakes would wake me. I would thrash my hands about, with the feeling that I was crashing or falling.

I had no desire to get back into a military plane, especially the C-141. I thought it was unsafe and just a matter of time before

I was killed. The sense that death was coming to take me was overwhelming.

I displayed signs of anxiety and post-traumatic stress, but did not identify with it. Drinking more was how I compensated. I had no desire to workout, and within ninety days of flying my last mission, I had put on twenty pounds. It didn't occur to me that what I had done during the war was affecting me. I had never fired a gun, was never wounded, never even felt like someone was shooting directly at me. I was a different person than I had been before the war.

Toward the end of August, my symptoms worsened. Things I used to do for relaxation made me anxious. I tried wakeboarding. I found that putting a life jacket on and getting in the water was terrifying. I couldn't take a deep breath. I had chest pain. I was wired tightly and could not calm down. I could not enjoy being with my friends or in large crowds.

Friends from the firefighting academy had a homecoming party on the waterfront. I looked for excuses, but finally showed up. Comrades were excited to see me and had several pitchers of beer on the table. We hugged and shook hands. I could not relax. I made my way through the bar, looking for threats and a safe place to sit. There were so many people shoulder to shoulder, just like on the plane. I sat facing the entrance of the bar, waiting for death to walk in.

My friends exchanged small talk when finally one of them asked, "How was it over there?"

The question that vets cringe at. How was it over there? Pondering. How do I answer such a question? The group at the table stopped to listen. Ears were focused. I let loose.

"It sucks over there. So many wounded. I never expected to see so many bodies. You're tired, you're hot, you can't keep up. . . . There is always another load of wounded waiting for you. And our leadership sucked. No support . . . I have no idea what we are fighting for. *There is no concept of winning from the inside of a medevac plane.*"

I looked up from my beer, and everyone was quiet. Uncomfortable silence. No one at home really wanted to know what it was like over there. I poured another beer and changed the subject, asking about tattoos.

I appreciated what my friends had tried to do. Confined spaces with people were too much like being on the jet again. I left the bar fairly sober, but drank more at home, regretting that I had said anything about what it was like over there. I went to bed to rest for the next round of arguments with Jennifer.

We got into fights over the war. Once again, I argued stupid things. I was quarrelling over a war that I had no control over. She had difficulty relating. Her war was over in six weeks. She had had good leadership. Jennifer flew in-country on C-130 turboprop planes. Her missions were significantly shorter with fewer patients. She stayed in one time zone and continent. We went to the same war with a similar mission. Her experience was significantly different. We did not understand each other.

I was attacking my best friend. During one argument, Jennifer reached over and tapped me on the back of the head. I stood up to hit her with all my might and stopped short. I recognized there was something wrong with me. I almost hit the woman I loved the most.

That night, Jennifer made a list of all my behavior changes. She handed me the list crying and said, "There's something wrong with you. You need to go talk to someone about this or our marriage isn't going to last." I knew she was right.

The next day, I made an appointment to see the flight surgeon. Before I went to the appointment, my twin, Eric, and friend AJ came over to talk. They verbally double-teamed me. Collectively they said, "If you got a problem with the war, fine. But don't take it out on your wife. She's too good to you and you know better. If you want to be mad, be mad, but don't drag Jennifer down with you. We don't want to hear again that you have been yelling at her over bullshit. If you need to yell at someone, call and you can yell at us." I knew they were right. I had to do something about it.

# August 22, 2003 *A truck bomb at the UN Headquarters kills the top UN envoy, Sergio Vieira de Mello, and twenty-one others. -CNN*

I reported to the flight surgeon, explaining how I felt. I was also having stomach problems. My GI tract was a mess, ranging from gastric reflux to an irritable bowel. The flight surgeon grounded me for my stomach and referred me over to the base psychologist. My crew thought I was removed from flight status for the Zantac I was taking, but the underlying reason was behavior.

A problem I had with the military psychologist was the forms I had to sign prior to the interview. They informed me that if I had done something wrong or out of line that they would have to report it to my commander.

So I toned down my behavior. I didn't tell them I was drinking every day, nor how much. I made sure not to say anything that would affect my career.

The Doc asked if I feared for my life while deployed. I said no. I didn't tell him what was eating at me inside. Something I did not identify till months, maybe years later. I could not get over the guilt I had from leaving soldiers behind. I made a conscious decision to leave wounded on the field of battle, to protect the lives of our crew, and the patients we already had loaded on the jet. I was not wounded, but I had a *moral injury* that would not heal.

I went through the routine with the doc. He wanted to know if I had any nightmares. I woke in the middle of the night with my heart racing and in a cold sweat. Jennifer would wake me from my nighttime mental fights. I rarely remembered the dreams. I had one dream that recurred enough to know every detail, down to each piece of field gear I was wearing and every wound I treated.

Jeremy, Tom, and I were in an underground maze, trying to find our way out. Around every corner that we turned there was a wounded soldier that needed care before we could move on. Of course, we'd never find our way out of the maze, and at every corner there was another body. The maze darkened and went downhill as we moved from body to body.

It was more than treating the wounded that got to me. It was the lack of control. We were micromanaged at every level. We had no control over the broken planes. No control over our lives. But most of all, we had no control over the volume of patients that kept coming. There was no light at the end of the dark, bloody tunnel.

After seeing so many men who were uniformed like me, I thought it was only a matter of time before I was injured or dead.

The psychologist was understanding and diagnosed me with combat fatigue. He said my condition was manageable, treatable, and not much worse than a bad case of burnout. He offered medication to get through the next couple of months. I refused. Psych meds would end my flying career. I had booze to help me on the bad days. I was grounded from flying (DNIFed) till the end of 2003.

Images that wake me up at night. The cost of war.

In September, Jennifer and I went to Cleveland, Ohio, to visit her parents. It was with extreme effort that I got on the commercial plane. When the flight attendant closed the hatch, I wanted to get up and run. The confined space filled with people was crushing. I could not take a deep breath. I ordered two drinks.

In Ohio, I talked to my father-in-law, a Vietnam vet who knew about war. Jim said it would take time and talked about combat and being shot in the face. Talking with someone who could relate to war was helpful.

That night, a Midwest thunderstorm rolled in and woke me. I rushed to the window and looked out at the lawn. With every flash of lightning, I saw insurgents moving from bush to bush. With the next bolt, they were gone . . . I stood at the window, paralyzed and utterly afraid. Jennifer called me back to the bed. I couldn't return to sleep.

I spent the fall working though my feelings and having regular appointments. I started exercising and cutting back on the pot of coffee I was drinking during the day. I gained some control.

Over time, the nightmares diminished. I still searched for sleep. I supplemented the drinking with Benadryl, or muscle relaxers to get four hours of sleep a night. Jennifer helped as much as she could. I talked to her less about what was going on in my head and acted better in front of her. She helped me through the toughest times when I first came home. I didn't want her to think I was still having problems. I was in her debt for not giving up. I could not blame her if she left.

# Discharged

## November 2003

*President Bush makes a stealthy Thanksgiving Day visit to Baghdad to boost morale among the troops and ordinary Iraqis. - CNN*

The month of November really changed my outlook. We were released from active duty. The Department of Defense reduced the number of involuntary recalled reservists. The senior leadership still thought victory was within reach. I thought it was hopeless.

On the same day I received my orders to deactivate, the ops officer requested we volunteer back onto active duty. A few people from my group volunteered to extend for one month. I told them, "You're going to regret that decision. They'll never get enough volunteers to fill all the open slots. Once the military realizes this, you will be involuntarily extended."

History proved me right. The volunteers were extended another year. The Pentagon came to the conclusion that victory was a goal to shoot for but not necessarily achieve.

I immediately requested a leave of absence from the Reserves. I had over sixteen years of military service. I needed a break, otherwise I might quit. The leave was granted, and I intended to take the next three months off before returning to civilian work as a firefighter.

My military health care would end, so I went to the Veterans Administration (VA) to enroll in their medical system. The VA offered two years of free medical to any Iraqi Freedom/Enduring Freedom veteran. I enrolled before the wave of returning veterans flooded the unprepared VA. I was seen within two weeks. It was not so easy with the paperwork.

I filed a claim for nightmares and the problems I was having with my gut. I could not make sense of the process. I was an educated registered nurse with a four-year bachelor's degree and could not understand how to navigate the VA bureaucracy. I had to seek help from the Veterans of Foreign Wars and the Order of the Purple Heart, volunteer groups that helped vets with the burdened VA system. They filed the claim for me. How does an eighteen-year-old with a high school education and a traumatic brain injury find the path through the VA?

I was relieved to have the two years of health care. It gave the slow-moving VA time to handle my paperwork. It was processed in eighteen months.

Stateside living made me miss the rush of adrenaline I'd get from flying missions. The thought of going back crossed my mind. I was bored and needed something to feel alive again.

It started to snow in the Cascade Mountains. Ski season was coming, and I could think of no better way to get my mind right.

Crystal Mountain opened in November. One of the earliest ski seasons in years. I skied two or three times a week. I found my adrenaline fix.

The alpine snow was the best tonic to cure my sleepless nights. I felt free in the mountains, and the powder-covered fir trees were the opposite of anything I had seen in the Middle East. I felt complete, happy, and in control of my life. After a solid day of skiing, I slept soundly at night. The days I did not ski, I had nightmares and still fought for a full night's rest.

The war continued both overseas and in my head. On November 22, a Dutch cargo plane was shot down by a SAM over Baghdad. The crew managed to crash-land the severely damaged plane. Luck and skilled airmanship kept them from being a smoking hole.

On December 10, one of our own planes, a C-17 from McChord AFB, was struck by a SAM while it took off out of Baghdad. I knew a loadmaster on the crew.

When he was home, I talked to Jim about the missile strike. He recounted the terror with wide eyes: "The number two engine exploded, blowing holes throughout the jet. It continued to burn even after we landed. Airport crash rescue had to extinguish the plane."

When the plane was ferried back to McChord, I went to the hangar and examined it. There were holes all over the left side of the fuselage from the nose gear back to the left troop door. I walked around inside the plane and saw where shrapnel had come through the thin skin of the jet. One passenger was wounded. I looked at the holes and thought about how lucky they had been . . . how lucky I had been.

In December, I sent out one final e-mail to everyone I had been writing:

> Thought I would give out a note on what's been happening since I got home from the war.
>
> The military, in its infinite wisdom, is trying to fill overseas assignments with volunteers. About twenty of us received notice to deactivate. We were then asked to volunteer to go back. I ran like the wind. They gave us thirty days to out-process and use up our leave. I was discharged from the active duty military and transferred back to the Air Force Reserve on Nov 24, 2003. I then promptly asked for a three-month leave of absence.

I'm not sure why I was released. I think it was a mistake, because I know we do not have enough people to cover the missions.

I'm taking the next three months off to get caught up with my civilian life and try to figure out who my wife is. Jennifer and I have only seen each other three out of the last ten months. We have some catching up to do.

I will be returning to my civilian job as a firefighter at the end of February 2004.

Jennifer is gone for six weeks at a military leadership school and will be returning home Dec. 15th.

I want you all to know that taking care of the wounded was the most rewarding and difficult experience of my life.

I am sorely disappointed by how we were treated by the active duty military. I felt the activated reservist was treated like a second-class citizen. I am therefore taking this time off to re-evaluate my role and career in the Air Force Reserve.

My hair has grown back after shaving my head. In fact, I have stopped shaving all together.

Thank you all for the support you gave me and my family during the war. Thank you for supporting my writing. I'm not 100% certain what I will do with the journal I wrote during the war. But I have started writing again. I am currently bridging the short stories together, so they make a complete book.

— Ed, looking for snow.

**December 1, 2003** *Iraq's deposed leader Saddam Hussein is captured by American troops. The former dictator was found hiding in a hole near his hometown of Tikrit and surrendered without a fight.- CNN*

On Christmas Day 2003, Jennifer and I skied on fresh powder. We ran into Jim Andrues and Jeff and Fran Sharp from Mountain Rescue. Over beers, Jim asked me to be his climbing partner for the annual February ice climbing trip in Canada. I had not been ice climbing in years. I jumped at the opportunity to be Jim's climbing partner. The mountains satisfied my need for adrenaline and helped me sleep.

# January 2004

In an effort to forget about the war and spend more quality time together, Jennifer and I went to La Ventana, Mexico, and camped on the beach. My brain was confused, fearing death and at the same time seeking adrenaline. I had crazy thoughts of returning to Iraq to find something I had lost. Life seemed so flat and without purpose.

We took kiteboarding lessons. Kiteboarding gave me the rush I sought. After a lesson, I was standing on the beach when a boarder came in close and asked for help landing his kite. He was riding a large, twelve-meter kite. It was gusty. He was wearing a helmet that marked him as a student. The hair stood up on my neck, alert to the fact that this guy was new to this sport, just like me. I cautiously walked to the shore and signaled him to lower the kite. As he lowered the kite to the beach, the amateur lost control. The rigid kite sliced through the air as a guillotine, missing my head by inches. I felt the rush of air blow my hair as the leading edge of the kite accelerated in front of me. It crashed into my left arm, driving my body to the ground and burying the arm in the sand. The pain was blinding.

That night my left arm swelled and changed color from tanned to dark blue, bruising. I drank a bottle of tequila to mask the pain. I never considered going to a Mexican hospital. We were hours from a city. I'd wait till I was home and flew back three days later.

Back home, our friend Elizabeth stopped by to hear about our trip. She immediately noticed my left arm and asked me to flex. I did, and my bicep flopped. "You ruptured your biceps tendon Ed. You need surgery."

Elizabeth was an ER doc at Madigan Army Medical Center on Ft. Lewis. She arranged for me to be seen in the ER the next day.

At the ER, two orthopedic surgeon residents looked at my arm and said I had a strain and to go home. Elizabeth did not agree. She called the staff attending surgeon at home and asked him to see me. He came in, did a few tests on my arm, and agreed that the tendon was ruptured. He also warned me that I had to have surgery within fourteen days or the tendon would atrophy, making surgery impossible. It was nine days since the accident. The staff surgeon tried to operate that day, but there was no room. He said I would get a call for surgery.

At day twelve, there was still no call. So I called the army hospital. My case had been lost in the maze of the military health care system. The clerk explained that I could get surgery in a week. I stressed that the surgery had to be done in the next forty-eight hours or I wouldn't be illegible for the repair. After a few more calls, I had the operation the next day. There went my ice climbing trip.

Reconstructive surgery ruined my last month of vacation. I was feeling down about myself. I made it through the war without a scratch only to get hit by a kite while on vacation.

*** 

Rehab was at Madigan. I shared a ward with combat veterans of Iraqi Freedom and Enduring Freedom. On clinic day, we would line up on gurneys in an open bay, and the surgeons would look at our wounds. We would talk about our injuries to each other. A gunner displayed what was left of his knee after an IED went off under his "deuce and a half" truck. The floorboard went through his leg.

"Where were you hit, buddy?" he said as he looked at my casted arm.

"La Ventana."

"Never heard of it? Is it in southern Iraq?"

"It's in western Mexico. Was on R&R."

"Oh."

Interacting with wounded soldiers brought the war back. It was therapeutic to talk to them. I also felt guilty for being safe at home. They were positive and upbeat about their combat wounds and thankful to be alive. I was upset about my Mexican injury.

Few of the combat wounds I saw in the orthopedic clinic looked like they were going to heal completely. My arm had a good chance of full recovery. I had plenty to be thankful for.

## February 2004 *Under pressure from both sides of the political aisle, President Bush calls for an independent commission to study the country's intelligence failures. - CNN*

The day my cast was removed was discouraging. My arm looked so small, atrophied, and deformed. I walked slump-shouldered to the prosthetic clinic and was fitted for a mechanical splint to wear for the next three months.

As I walked down the hall, a very young GI was hobbling the other direction. His tan face and high and tight haircut pegged him as an Iraqi Freedom veteran. He was receiving training on how to use crutches. The solider was excited and animated to be up and moving. I walked past and noticed he was missing his right leg below the knee.

At that point, my arm did not seem so deformed. My injury was small and insignificant compared to that leg. The GI's thrilled smile was an added source of inspiration.

Though I had problems getting in the military medical system, once in I was well taken care of. Most of the vets I talked to were happy with their care. Getting in was the hard part.

That night, the phone rang at 10:30 p.m. We were ready for bed and let the phone ring. I had an autonomic response anytime I heard the ringer, especially at odd hours. We were alerted for medevac missions by phone. My cranium equated a phone ringing to flying another mission. I fought my brain and picked up the phone.

"Ed, its Jeff Sharp. Jim Andrues and John Miner are missing up in Canada. They found their car and not far up the trail a large avalanche pile. We are taking the mountain rescue team up to look for them. Do you want to go?"

I didn't know how to react. After I ruptured my arm, I had to cancel out on the trip. Jim went to Canada without me for ice climbing. Jim could not find another climbing partner and ended up driving by himself. In Canada, he tagged onto John's rope team.

I responded, "Jeff, I had surgery on my arm and can't use it. I'm pretty useless. Let me call you back after I talk this over with Jennifer. Give me ten minutes."

I felt anxiety. I'd survived the war, narrowly missed getting my head whacked in Mexico, and now my climbing partner was most likely dead on the rope I was expected to be attached to. It appeared I was dodging death. I talked with Jennifer. Realizing I only had use of one arm and was hopped up on narcotics, I was useless to the rescue team. I had not been on a mission with Tacoma Mountain Rescue in three years. Yet Jim and John were my friends and I couldn't leave them in the snow.

I called Jeff back, told him I'd meet the team at the rally point. Maybe I could help run base operations or a radio relay. Jennifer packed my bags.

We met at the rescue cache, and the team was loading equipment into trucks. Avalanche poles, shovels, and distress beacons. We went through the motions, yet somehow I knew that our friends were dead. The chances of survival buried in an avalanche drop to zero after twenty minutes.

It took us twelve hours to drive to Banff National Park in the interior of Canada. By the time we had arrived, climbing rangers had found the bodies of our friends, including Russ Howard, a man I had not met.

We drove to where Jim's truck was parked and then hiked the short walk to the avalanche debris. Rocky Mountain House Rescue was our escort and narrated what had happened.

"Your friends were ice climbing just off the road. The accident happened between 2:00 and 3:00 p.m. as temps in the area warmed up with afternoon sun. The three were climbing a route called *Midnight Rambler*, an ice climb that has an eighty-degree grade and is considered a challenging route suited for experienced climbers. At about 7:00 p.m., the other climbers from the party went looking for the three men after they failed to turn up at the lodge. They went to the waterfall, and that's where they found the avalanche, a rope, and a helmet. They contacted Parks Canada. We don't feel the avalanche was caused by your friends. When you look up high, there are slabs that were pulled out, so it's likely a naturally triggered avalanche from the heat of the day yesterday. At the time of the accident, the temp in the climbing area was minus fifteen Celsius, while on top of the mountain temperatures hit minus one Celsius as the sun hit the upper slopes. The avalanche swept down the gully, and the debris field measured five meters deep, making searching difficult. Park wardens and rescue personnel were on scene by midnight Thursday, searching for the climbers using probes and two avalanche dogs and handlers from Jasper and Banff. Within minutes, an avalanche dog found one climber. The search continued until about 3:00 a.m. and resumed at about 6:30 a.m. Friday.

"The second climber was found by 9:00 a.m., and the body of the third was recovered by 10:30 a.m. Friday morning. We found them in one-point-five, two, and four meters of snow."

I was in awe. My friends never knew what hit them. They never heard the slide that started thousands of feet above. The only warning they may have had was the shock wave of air that preceded the wall of snow. They were dead before the snow had settled.

We stood over the blood-tinged snow pile. Friends cried, mourned, and said prayers for our brothers. I was mystified at the majestic landscape that they enjoyed. They died in the mountains they cherished.

That night, Tacoma Mountain Rescue stayed with Rocky Mountain House Rescue. We were a pitiful group depressed in our own sorrow. I needed a drink. I grabbed a driver, and we headed out into wintered countryside. Luckily, in Canada there was no problem finding a late night liquor store in the middle of isolated mountains. I bought several bottles of scotch, gin, and tonic.

We got back to the house, and I announced to the group, "Our friends are dead. We can't change that. They died doing what we all love. Jim and John would be pissed if they saw how morbid we were. Let's celebrate their lives. Honor them and drink with me."

We proceeded to get drunk, toasting our friends over and over. I mixed in some of my pain medicine to shake the feeling that the Grim Reaper was grabbing a toe.

Late into the night, we finally bedded down. Nightmares of avalanches and war woke me. The booze and narcs could not keep me asleep. It was 4:00 a.m. and I found myself outside, staring at the stars in minus fifteen-degree weather, feeling a chill that was certainly death. I walked through the snow, wondering why I was awake, just like I'd done at Bastogne, Switzerland, Skagway, and Germany.

We sobered up, headed home, and buried our friends.

# March 2004

It had been a year since I'd worked as a firefighter. I returned to my civilian job mentally and physically damaged. The fire department had also changed. While I was overseas, the fire chief was arrested and convicted for heroin use. The department was a shambles. Morale was exceptionally low, and the city was wrestling to clean the mess. I returned to work in time for a going away party: two firefighters had had enough and had moved to another department. I could have joined them, but had missed the opportunity to test while overseas.

I was assigned a desk next to the temporary chief. Richard had been hired to salvage and overhaul the department. He was in his seventies and had over forty years in the fire service. We established an immediate respect for each other from our life experiences. Richard also buried me with office work.

I gave my best effort to help out, but I hated office life. The more I worked at the desk, the more I wanted to leave the fire department. Paperwork did not provide the excitement I'd known overseas.

I spent the next four months working three days a week. My off time was spent rehabbing my arm and getting my life in order. I needed a new direction to go. I wanted my head straight.

I joined a support group at the Veterans Center in Tacoma. The counselor and group therapy helped sort my mind. I realized that I wasn't alone in how I felt or acted. There were other vets worse off. The counselor encouraged us to talk about our fears. As before, it wasn't fear that bothered me, it was guilt. I realized that I transposed my guilt into anger.

After a couple of months, a new veteran joined the group. I didn't recognize him except for the distinctive zippered Z scar on his forehead. I told him, "You were injured in Iraq working on heavy equipment and then medevac'd to Spain in the spring of '03."

"Yeah, how'd know? "

"Because I'm the nurse that took care of you."

We locked eyes, shook hands, and hugged. Rodney thanked me profusely for helping him. I could see he was still having problems with his head injury. We talked about the war and our lives now. He was unemployed, unable to return to his well-paying job as a heavy equipment operator. Rodney was struggling to provide for his family, dealing with headaches, anger, and no income. I went home wishing I could do more for him. Guilt was a feeling that I couldn't shake.

My arm healed enough to return to duty as a firefighter. I'd been back to work long enough to understand that small-town fire department life was not working. I was not challenged and was bored with the uninteresting calls. Getting a cat out of a tree or helping the inept who had locked their keys in the car did not have the same excitement level as caring for sixty to eighty wounded at a time. I needed something more stimulating.

Though my arm had little strength, I tested and passed the candidate physical ability test (CPAT), a fitness test that fire departments use for hiring. The test was not challenging except in hiding the fact that I did the course with only one good arm. My name made it to the hire list of several fire departments.

Come fall, our medevac squadron was asked to deploy again, voluntarily. The war continued on, and every six months the Pentagon came up with a new plan to manage the personnel shortages. Headquarters' sales pitch was that if enough people volunteered for four months of overseas duty, they would not have to involuntarily recall reservists for a year. There was this optimistic thought that the war would be over soon, though there was no sign from the battlefield.

Jennifer volunteered for another deployment. She crewed medevac out of Germany. Leaving just before Christmas, we continued to move farther apart. I focused on improving my strength and fitness for a new job.

My arm though healed, kept me grounded in the Reserves. The flight surgeon marked in my record, "No flying duty assignments or field conditions." He explained, "We won't accept the liability of you lifting a two-hundred-pound marine and blowing your bicep again."

That was it; my military career was over. There was not much point in staying in the Air Force Reserve if I couldn't fly. I had lost faith in our senior military leadership and the Bush administration. I felt the war in Iraq was a (terrible waste of precious life) mistake.

I could no longer do a mission that I did not believe in. I also wanted a job at a larger fire department and knew that being a reservist would be a detriment for hiring.

I transferred to the inactive Reserve to ride out the last years before retirement. The timing was perfect. I had an interview at a large, progressive fire department. In the interview, the fire chief asked, "What is your status in the Reserves?" I did not like the question, but I wanted the job and did not argue.

"My career in the Reserves is almost over. I'm retiring."

I was also asked, "What are the chances of being mobilized?"

"There is no chance of me going back."

I got the job.

# Life Moves On, So Does the War

## January 2005

*The White House announces that the search for weapons of mass destruction in Iraq, one of the main justifications for the war, is officially over. No such weapons were found. -CNN*

Jennifer was gone, and I was in a sixteen-week recruit academy for my new job. I was so busy with training that I felt single. I had little time to talk to Jennifer and focused on the weekly grind of being a firefighter recruit. Our phone calls were short and awkward.

There was no time for the Vet Center. My weeks were consumed with firefighter training. I still had problems with sleeping, anxiety, a short temper, and this fear that death was following me. The intense physical training left me exhausted. The harder I trained, the better I slept at night. I confided in three of my classmates that I was a vet still dealing with what I had done and seen. I asked them to keep an eye on me, keep me out of trouble, especially my short temper. I also apologized in advance for my temper. Danika, Ryan, and Billy replaced the group therapy at the Vet Center. They listened to me and helped me continue my adjustment to civilian life. They became hard-fast friends who I counted on.

# May 2005

We were close to end of academy. The rigorous school made me think less about the war and more about my civilian life. It gave transition and focus. I still had this intense fear of death and remained hyper-vigilant all through academy. Live fire training killed my dread of the Grim Reaper.

Our class was assigned to burn down an abandoned home. The instructors would set small fires, and we would extinguish them. There were extensive safety standards to follow, and everyone knew it was training and not an unpredictable fire with unknown hazards. Each subsequent fire was burned longer to challenge the recruits.

Ryan, Billy, and I were in a squad assigned to attack a simulated basement fire. Basement fires are dangerous because there are few windows or doors to ventilate the extreme heat and trapped gases.

The fire was set on the first floor, and we placed a ladder to gain access via the second floor, thus creating a basement. The first floor was sealed to provide a basement-like environment.

The three of us climbed up the ladder and entered the smoke-filled second story. As soon as we were in, we lost sight of each other. I was on the nozzle and Billy was right behind me, acting as eyes and ears to find the seat of the fire. Ryan was a few feet behind us, yarding in the heavy fire hose. We inched along the wall, looking for the stairs down to the fire. The heat drove us to hug the floor. We sucked air from our masks at a rapid rate. This was the hottest fire I'd ever been in. I bumped into something.

Unable to see, the object felt like a body. It was a training mannequin to simulate a victim. I crawled past the dummy, looking for the stairs. Ryan grabbed the mannequin and it stuck to the floor. The room was so hot that carpet melted to the dummy and our gloves. Ryan was able to get our victim out of the room only after melted carpet latched to his bunker gear.

I slid my hand forward and found the stairs. The stairwell was acting as a chimney, and hot fire gases were pumping up through the passageway. I stayed just outside the column of heat. Checking the nozzle and making sure it was in a fog pattern, I yelled that I was going down the stairs. The instructor said to wait until I could see flame.

I necked my face towards the stairs and edged into hell. I couldn't see, but I could feel the heat through the facemask. The temp increased, and an orange radiance developed before me. It was evil. It was death. The blaze outlined the shape of the stairwell. Flames were now visible, torching the carpet and licking in front of my face. The instructor yelled, "*Go, go, go, get down that stairwell!*"

I opened the bail to the nozzle with a water fog that created a protective curtain against the fire. Billy and I slid down the stairs on the melted carpet. Ryan stayed at the top of the stairs, feeding hose pressurized at a hundred PSI. The instructor followed us and called on the radio for the ventilation crew to open a hole to allow the hot gases to escape. The water pumped on the fire was expanding 1,700 times as it converts to steam. If we didn't clear the gases out quickly, we could be steam-burned.

Reaching the bottom of the stairs, I pressed my body flat trying to get below the heat. The matting on the ground floor had completely burned away, and we were prostrate on hot concrete. The instructor was yelling in the radio, "*Ventilate, ventilate...we need ventilation now!*" There was no response from the outside.

I could not see the fire and was spraying the water throughout the room. The intense heat was everywhere. I could feel my skin smoldering. I turned the hose on myself. It only made the burns worse as the water converted to steam.

At that moment, I became quite composed. I had the realization that I would burn to death and there was not a damn thing I could do to stop it. I looked the Grim Reaper in the face. He could take me now.

A hand grabbed my right shoulder. It was Billy. He yelled into my ear, "*Fire to your right!*"

I crawled forward and could see the seat of the fire. I adjusted my nozzle to a thirty-degree pattern and blasted the fire. The steam was still trapped in the room, and we were burning. I rolled onto my side and saw a sliver of daylight. I was up against the base of the fire and directly under a covered skylight. I changed the water pattern to a straight steam and punched a hole though the skylight.

Steam and hot fire gases rushed past me and out through the hole. I moved the water stream to open the hole. Drywall and particleboard fell on top of me. The larger hole gave us the daylight and ventilation we needed. Raining water extinguished the fire. I again adjusted my nozzle pattern to a fog, covering most of the hole. This increased the rate at which the fire gases left the room. The room quickly cooled. We could see, and we were alive. I looked back at Billy and the instructor. They were covered in soot, and steam ascended from their bunker gear. I looked down at my own body and saw steam rising from arms, legs, and chest. I lay on the floor, exhausted and content. I no longer feared death.

We put out the secondary fires and exited the building. The four of us removed our masks and firefighting gear. My helmet visor was stuck—warped from the heat. We were grinning at each other. That was one hot fire. I sat there for several minutes, sucking water, waiting for my heart rate to drop.

I was worn out. I was also free.

I no longer feared death because I now understood. I had no control over death. There was no reason to worry about it. The mental demon was gone. It had been burned out of me. The adrenaline wore off and I relaxed.

I slowly stood up and recognized that I'd been burned. There were small burns on my face and hands. It wasn't until I arrived home and showered that I recognized the extent of the damage. The hot water uncovered the second-degree blisters I had on my hands, face, neck, and the backs of my knees. I fumbled with the knobs to the cold water.

I went to bed but couldn't sleep. They were little burns, but they were excruciating. I was a pussy compared to the severely burned soldiers I had treated. They never complained about the pain or the severe disfigurement.

I couldn't take it anymore. I got up, took two Percocet and waited for the narcotic to release me.

## Summer 2005 *The insurgency in Iraq is "in the last throes," Vice President Dick Cheney says, and he predicts that the fighting will end before the Bush administration leaves office. - CNN*

Jennifer was home from her volunteer, four-month deployment. I was happy at work and thought it was time for us to work on our marriage. The air force had other plans. The scheme of getting volunteers did not work. There were not enough suckers. Jennifer was involuntarily recalled for another year of active duty. She was told the four-month tour she just completed didn't count toward her mobilization because she had volunteered.

I was furious at the military and angry at Jennifer. It was not her fault, but who else could I take it out on? Our marriage continued to crack and strain. We had by then spent so much time apart that we had lost the ability to communicate with each other.

Jennifer deployed for the third time. I was now the dependent husband at home. Luckily, we had no children that suffered through this. I contemplated single life. We had only seen each other eighteen months out of three years. The time together was strained, and the strain was mainly my fault.

I enjoyed my new job and got the excitement I sought at the larger fire department. I was alive fighting fire. As a new employee, I didn't have a choice in assignments and was scheduled to drive the medic unit. I worked with a paramedic and acted as the assistant. It was a role reversal for me, because I was used to having medics work for me on the plane. I didn't mind following orders.

The paramedics were professional and experienced. I no longer had a love for medicine.

It had been two years since I had treated a critical patient, and there was nothing to excite me in the back of the medic unit. A trauma patient or cardiac arrest had little effect on me. It seemed mundane after caring for sixty-some patients at once. Medical calls are one patient, and we have plenty of help compared to the cramped medevac planes. Occasionally a call stirred memories.

We responded to a pedestrian hit by a car. It was dark and raining, and the driver never saw the young woman crossing the road. The fire engine blocked the crowded intersection. I saw the woman down in the center of the road. I walked up, looking for other cars that might hit us. The medic ordered me to stabilize her head and neck. I knelt down into a pool of blood, holding her head with my hands. My left hand sank into a bloody mess where her skull was depressed and fractured . . .

Flash –

I was back on the jet, kneeling over a patient, ready to start an IV. I was working in the humid darkness of the cabin floor and smelled human toil and the enclosed mechanical stench of the plane . . .

Flash –

I was back in the middle of the road, looking into the terrified eyes of the woman. I hesitated as I refocused between the present and the past. As I held her head and life in my hands, I told her firmly, "Listen to me, you are hurt but are going to be okay. I promise you that none of the firefighters here are going to let anything happen to you. You are safe with us." Her eyes smiled and relaxed. We loaded her in the medic unit, and she lived.

Back at the station, I laid in my bunk, staring at the ceiling. Damn it. I had had a flashback. It scared the hell out of me and sleep escaped me. It was the only time I've ever had a flashback, and I prayed that it didn't occur again.

I requested assignment on the fire engine and avoided working on the medic unit.

During late fall, I engrossed myself in firefighting, and Jennifer worked her staff job in Germany. She coordinated the patient movement out of Iraq. She was also assigned the duty of overseeing the movement of the dead. The military, always using acronyms, used to refer to our war dead as KIAs. It's now fashionable to refer to them at HRs.

I talked to Jennifer on the phone and listened. She was starting to sound like me. The volume of dead and wounded continued to increase. As a staff officer, she could now see the big picture compared to one small planeload of wounded. Jennifer sent out an e-mail in frustration.

### HR

I'm on my third overseas deployment as a mobilized reservist since the Iraq war began in March 2003. This time I work in the Aeromedical Evacuation Operations Cell (AEOC) in the Air Mobility Control Center (AMCC), on Ramstein Air Base, Germany. To enter the door to my workplace at the AMCC, I must first turn off and stow my cell phone/pager, punch in a code, check behind me for strangers, and then proceed through the door labeled, "WARNING-Controlled Area." Inside the AMCC, which is surrounded on 3 sides by windows overlooking the flight line, 3 stories up, there are 6 different sections, 25 yelling people (active duty and activated reservists/guardsmen), 50 computer screens, 50+ phones, 6 doorbells, 20 Motorola radios, and 5 plasma screens. Not only are these technological items ringing, squawking, beeping all day long, every second of the day, they heat up our 30' X 30' room to a nice 85 degrees, not sure why the air conditioning can't keep up! We are all deployed here for one reason, to support the Global War on Terrorism.

At the top of our tree are the AMCC controllers, they control each and every aircraft that come in and out of Ramstein. They talk directly to the pilots and relay information down to

each of the 5 sections. One branch is the Air
Terminal Operations Center; these guys control
the cargo and passengers on and off the planes.
The maintenance section lets us know if any of
our planes are broke or require maintenance.
The C-17 stage managers control their front end
crews and missions to the Areas of Operation
of Iraq, Afghanistan, and the other "Stans."
The other C-17 stage managers are my counter
parts; they are activated Jackson Guard members
from MS who fly only the med-evac missions. The
vast majority of the medevac mission is managed
and flown by mobilized Guard and Reservists. I
control and oversee the Aeromedical missions
and patients that come in and out of Ramstein
from Iraq and Afghanistan. All 6 sections work
together to launch and recover missions from
our desks, relaying messages and giving orders
to our folks who are down on the flight line
performing the hands-on part of our jobs.

Our days are non-stop . . . people yelling
across the room, spouting out tail numbers,
Zulu times, ETICs, ICAO codes, delays, cargo,
passenger numbers, alpha numbers, spot #'s,
weather forecasts, all over radios, telephones
and to one another. The days can be so crazy,
the volume so loud and stressful that you can
feel the tension in the air. At times, I have
considered jumping out the window! Again, we are
all here for Operation Iraqi Freedom and Enduring
Freedom; we are the hub for every mission coming
out of Iraq and The "Stans," and the hub for
every mission going to the states. We are not
on the forefronts of the battle, or in harms
way, but we all have come to the realization
that there is a war going on down there and has
been going on for 4 years now. We realize this
because of 2 letters . . . HR . . . Hotel Romeo.

I hear or see the letters "HR" every day that I
work, sometimes 50 or more times a day. I hear

HR over the radio, I see it on checklists on the fax machine, on the computers, on the plasma screen, or I see it with my own eyes on the flight line. Perhaps, it is the same HR I see or hear 30 times a day, but each section gets word of the HR and the information gets relayed many times over. "4 HR's, 8 HR's, or 3 HR's, it does not matter, each time I hear the letters HR, I cringe, I think about whom the HR may be, who's son or daughter, father or mother, or spouse. I look to see if I recognize the name of the HR, and I am usually selfishly relieved that it is not a HR I personally know. But someone personally knows, cares or loves this HR.

Though we are not in the desert, fighting in the sand and heat, all of us here at AMCC are affected by this war. We are away from our families for months and years. It is time lost that we will never get back. Most of all, we are deeply moved and forever changed by our most solemn duty; arranging and executing the final journey of our valiant precious cargo, our HR's.

Coincidence . . . just as I finished writing this letter, I stepped to the window to watch the offload of my patients from the C-17. As I stood there at the window, 9 HR's rolled by on a K-loader truck to be loaded into the back of a C-5, heading to Dover Air Force Base, DE. Each HR, had a perfect tightly wrapped American flag around each casket. Three HR's per pallet were loaded respectfully and professionally by the Air Terminal representatives and the loadmasters of the mission, only touching the pallet with their hands and never touching Old Glory. Our HR's, our heroes, are returning home.

**HR=Human Remains**

Major Jennifer Hrivnak

5 November 2005

Jennifer understood what I had been feeling those last two years. She invited me to see her in Germany. It was a chance to patch up our marriage.

*\*\*\**

December 2005 *Iraq holds parliamentary elections. As many as eleven million Iraqis turn out to select their first permanent Parliament since the overthrow of Saddam Hussein. More than seven thousand Parliamentary candidates from three hundred parties are seeking to fill the 275 seats in Parliament. Violence is minimal. - CNN*

I went to Germany for ten days of vacation with Jennifer. The polar flight was without incident. I still felt anxiety on the plane and nervously checked the passenger and escape hatches. I actually napped on the plane.

Our ten days together were healing. We escaped to Austria for a few days on a second honeymoon of skiing, dancing, and loving. We had a new perspective of each other. There was hope for our marriage. It was the first time we had talked to each other as partners in a long time.

On a day Jennifer had to work, I walked the air base and noticed a medevac plane land. I hitched a ride to the flight line and observed the wounded being off-loaded. It had been three years since I'd flown my first combat mission. Not much had changed. No end in sight. The wounded kept pouring off the plane. I was sickened by what I saw. There was nothing I could do to change what was happening. The war was a mistake, churning forward, grinding bodies, and no one was able to stop it.

# January 2006

Jennifer was home from her third deployment. She was different this time and was stressed. The war had gotten to her and I saw myself in her. The air force offered an early release from her twelve-month mobilization and she took it. She was pregnant.

We were excited and saw this as a chance to start again, but then she had a miscarriage. Our world came crashing down, and neither one of us dealt with it very well. We took it out on each other. The strain of three years of war and a poor marriage finally cracked. We couldn't go on like this. We looked for reasons for the miscarriage.

Was it the stress of the war? Was it the damn anthrax shots we were forced to take? Whose fault was it? It didn't matter. Our child was gone. Jennifer was increasingly aggressive and agitated. I then knew what it was like to live with myself. It was a complete role reversal. I made a contingency plan to move out of the house and ask for marriage counseling. I also suggested to Jennifer that she was having problems with the war. She yelled that she didn't need help, that she was not one of *those people*.

After a few more weeks, Jennifer exploded because I changed some of the furniture and threw out stuff while she was gone.

"Life does not stop when you're overseas. I can't wait for you to come home to make decisions."

She yelled back, "When I want something done, I expect it to be done my way the first time!"

"Listen here major, you are not deployed in your staff job right now and I'm not your subordinate. I don't follow orders from you!"

We continued to fight, and it led nowhere. After a few days of cooling down, we nervously attended marriage counseling and grief therapy for the miscarriage.

The sessions forced us to communicate. What really helped was spending time together. We had the foundation for a good relationship. We needed time with each other to make it work. We relearned how to talk as a couple and not a military unit. The year 2006 marked the first time in three years that we had the entire year together. We saved our marriage. Another deployment would have meant divorce.

Captain's Jennifer and Ed Hrivnak on a C-17 *Globemaster III* static display
set up for an air force TV commercial. This was prior to my retirement.
Keeping it together through difficult times.

*In a nationally televised address, President Bush announces an additional twenty thousand troops will be deployed to Baghdad to try to stem the sectarian fighting. He also says Iraq will take control of its forces and commit to a number of "benchmarks," including increasing troop presence in Baghdad and passing oil-revenue-sharing and jobs-creation plans.*

*The tally of death certificates and reports from morgues, hospitals, and other institutions indicates more than thirty-four thousand Iraqi civilians died in 2006.*

*- CNN*

# Epilogue

## 2008

It had been five years since the start of the second Iraq War. I felt somewhat normal again. Our lives would never be the same after what we went though. We were forever changed from the day we watched the Twin Towers fall on 9/11.

We were the lucky ones. Our marriage survived, and our relationship was stronger than before. We were alive and came home without physical injuries. The mental wounds had slowly healed and left scars. There were nights that I was up at 4:00 a.m. I stared at the ceiling wishing I could get back to sleep. Occasionally, the sullen eyes of wounded peered out from dreams. Jennifer nudged me to stop whimpering as I wrestled with bed sheets. It was a small price to pay.

I think of families that had paid with the lives of loved ones. I think of relationships and marriages that had been destroyed by this war. I have seen both sides. Home was just as difficult for families left behind. They were provided little support from the government.

I retired from the Air Force Reserve after twenty years of faithful service. At my retirement, one hundred and forty friends and family came to honor me (or maybe it was the free drinks). It was fitting closure. Many of them still serve, and I am awed at their continued sacrifice. Even now a small part of me feels guilt, knowing that so many of my comrades are still on the line defending my freedom, while I sit safely at home. I think of my crew often.

Tom still serves as a flight nurse and holds the squadron record for deployments. He has a record for number of patients evaced. He's been promoted, and I'm impressed at his commitment.

Jeremy quit being a medic, having had enough. He retrained as a loadmaster on the C-17 and now crews intercontinental and combat missions. Tom, Jeremy, and I get together every few months, toast the fallen, and boast our exploits and drunken memories. Reliving the early days of war when we truly felt we were making a difference and winning. We are tired, middle-aged veterans now.

Jimmy quit being a medic. Now he is a C-17 pilot, flying internationally with an entire crew and plane under him. I saw a leader in him the first day I met him in Sicily. He did not let us down. He is happily married and has started a family.

Robert still serves in the Reserves as a flight medic, though retirement knocks on his door. He juggles his civilian job as a health inspector, busy family life, and the increasing demands of the military on the traditional reservist. His unit is ready for another tour of duty. I do not hear from him often, but when I do it warms my soul.

Steve retired from the Reserves and still works as a mental health counselor. Like many of us, he had to adjust to civilian life and reintegrate with his family. I hear from Steve infrequently. He is still a voice of reason.

Cathleen called me one day. I had not talked to her in a year. She read my published stories in the book *Operation Homecoming* and understood she was not alone.

"The boy with the missing toes and sand fleas in his wounds was my patient. I was so busy with wounded . . . never made it to him. I saw you and Steve caring for him. I pressed on, but always felt guilt."

I never thought about him as her patient. A good crew takes care of each other when overwhelmed.

She carried guilt for years along with the intense feeling of never being able to do enough for the wounded. She too was touched by their sacrifices and could no longer work as a clinical nurse. Cathleen became homeless and unemployed. She had nightmares, depression, contemplated suicide, and lived with a black shroud over her life. She welcomed death.

Two years of lifting wounded and heavy medical bags destroyed the tendons in the elbows of her tiny frame. She lives in intense pain and has restricted use of her arms for hands-on care. Cathleen asked for help from the military, was ignored, and was pushed aside. She retired from the Reserves in disgust.

We talked for an hour, and I convinced her to seek help at the VA. She is now on medication for the nightmares and PTSD. Her claim is still pending for her elbows. My heart understands the despair she feels.

Cathleen told me the words I had written helped her to step forward and ask for help. She convinced me to finish this book. Maybe others coming home from the war will realize they are not alone. Perhaps others will seek help.

Cathleen now has a job at the VA as an intake nurse for returning combat veterans. She is a survivor.

On March 31, 2008, the seven of us met in Riverside, California to mark the five-year anniversary of our first combat mission and the day we initially met. We were hosted by Rick Binkley and Bobbie Pederson, the crusty flight engineers that kept our plane airborne. We had not been together as a crew since Spain in May of 2003.

We drank and joked about our escapades in crew rest and exploring Europe. Very little was said about the wounded or our challenges. I showed them the film clip *Medevac Missions* from the documentary *Operation Homecoming*. I said, "Thank you for your contribution. What I wrote is a tribute to your efforts and our patients."

A quiet room after the film stopped. All lost in thoughts. Finally, Steve looked up from his drink and stated, "I have to admit I've been in a sort of depression since coming home."

That broke the ice, and we openly talked about how we had changed from the war. None of us came back whole. All were working hard to reconstruct our lives and strengthen our families.

We hoped the patients brought home were able to do the same. I was provided with a snapshot of life after injury.

Rodney, my former patient I met at the Vet Center, crossed paths with me at the grocery store. The VA had retrained him into a new career and helped him and his family get back on track. He still suffered from the traumatic brain injury, headaches, and PTSD. He said, "I will never be the same in my head, but I have learned how to live with it. Life goes on."

Jennifer was resilient enough to stay when I was an asshole. She had her own demons to deal with coming home. She weathered it all, was promoted, and has several years until retirement. Through all of this, she was able to give our family a son, John Dawson.

I hope he will understand how fragile life is and cherish it. He brought new meaning to our marriage and has energized my soul.

My worst fear is that war will still be raging when Dawson is old enough to enlist. Jennifer and I are third-generation military to serve during war. I wish that my son doesn't follow our footsteps. I don't want him to see what we've lived. I wish that he never has to make decisions about who lives and who gets left behind. I hope and pray that when he becomes an adult that humans will have figured out how to live without war.

At the end of 2008, Jennifer gave birth to Shae Marie. Our daughter exudes unconditional love and affection. She's papa's girl. Shae has brought joy to our lives, healed wounds, and strengthened our marriage. I see good humanity through her eyes and actions.

What have I learned from this experience?

I've learned that the American soldier's spirit is a tough thing to break. You can put a GI in an unforgiving desert and deprive him of sleep, food, water, and shelter. Take away creature comforts such as a bed, a shower, a woman, or even a change of clothes. Mortar him, shoot at him, and ambush him. You can even wound him, tear open his lung, blow away an eyeball, or amputate an extremity. Capture her, torture and abuse her, and she will still come out on top. You can do all of these things and still not destroy the GI's spirit.

But if you wound or kill a trooper's buddy, his spirit falters. The love that comrades in arms have is stronger than the love between husband and wife. It is devotion equal to that between a mother and son. Friendships bonded in the crucible of war are the hardest things to break. They are most painful when broken in combat.

I have learned that if the people the soldier defends do not stand behind him as he fights *their* war; then his spirit is easily broken. A lack of support at home is an effective weapon to destroy an army.

I do not know how these wars are going to end, if ever. We have left Iraq, though American mercenaries and military advisors are still there in harms way. IED's still kill. We are leaving Afghanistan with no clear victory. Thousands of brothers and sisters in uniform are serving in brush-fire wars that are not talked about (Philippines, Pakistan, Yemen, and Africa).

My view is one-sided. I have never seen cities liberated or a foreign culture voting for the first time. I have never witnessed oppressed people freed. I have only seen war from the inside of a plane filled with wounded and lost friends. I have seen the worst of humanity represented by fractured bodies and souls. I have also seen the best of humankind, the wounded soldier that cares not of himself, but only the comrades that he served with. Even with the acts of courage and sacrifice I have witnessed, I see no glory in war.

# Acknowledgements

Thank you to my friends and family that encouraged and supported me.

Thank you Heidi Robinson, who taught me that being an author is more than just writing. It is a profession with its own set of rules.

Thank you Andy Carroll. You have opened my eyes to a world I knew little about: literature. Thank you for the education and friendship.

Thank you Jennifer, for not giving up on me.

# Glossary

**AEOT:** Aeromedical evacuation operations team. A sixteen-to thirty-two-person team that coordinates medevac ground operations at forward locations. Located well behind the front lines.

**AELT:** Aeromedical evacuation liaison team. A small team of three to six medical personnel that coordinate evac at more forward and austere locations. Usually work directly with the army and forward deployed ground forces. Work closer to the front line.

**AB:** Air base. An overseas location.

**AFB:** Air force base. A stateside location.

**AMBUS-** A standard school bus converted to carry litter patients.

**AOR:** Area of responsibility. The polite military term for the war zone. Better known as "the combat zone," "the box," or "the battlefield." Senior military officers like to use the term AOR because "war zone" has such a negative meaning. AOR sounds nonthreatening, like going to the IGA to buy food.

**ALPHA Alert:** A crew standing by to be airborne within one hour.

**Battle Buddies:** a term used by the military to designate the pairing of individuals. It is taught at basic training to instill teamwork so no one works alone.

**Back-end Crew:** The crew in the back of the plane. The medical crew not part of flying the aircraft.

**BRAVO Alert:** A crew standing by to be airborne in three hours.
**Beretta, or Nine Mil:** The issued side arm for any aircrew member. It holds fifteen nine milimeter rounds and is used for self defense.
**BX:** Base Exchange. On base store, like a military version of Target.
**CHARLIE Alert:** A crew standing by to be airborne in twelve hours.
**CCATT:** Critical care air transport team. A highly specialized team of a doctor, nurse, and respiratory therapist that cares for the most critical patients. Patients that would have died during the first Gulf War now live thanks to advances in medicine and this team's incredible skill.
**Civvies:** Civilian clothing.
**CMC:** Crew management cell. A small group of flyers that organize and manage the flying crews. They control the day-to-day launch and recovery of the medevac missions.
**Chief Nurse:** The senior nurse within the squadron who manages nurses. Makes decisions on nurse-to-patient ratio and manages nursing care standards. Addresses patient care issues, not operations.
**C-5:** The *Galaxy*. The largest transport in the US Air Force. The plane is for oversized cargo.
**C-141:** The *Starlifter* was the air cargo workhorse of the air force. It was designed and built in the early 1960s. The plane that numbered in the hundreds during the first Gulf War was reduced to about fifty-four decades-old aircraft. Age and lack of spare parts made the aircraft unreliable. The last airframe was retired in 2006 at the air force museum. Most aircraft were chopped for scrap. A few complete examples can be found on lawns as historical memories at military bases.
**C-17:** The *Globemaster III* is the newest airlifter in the air force inventory. The jet has the ability to fly heavy outsized cargo to austere forward locations. It has the ability to land and take off on short, unimproved dirt airfields. The drawback to the plane is that it was brand new and there were not enough of them. It was also lacking in equipment to be fully utilized for Aeromedical evacuation missions (AMEs).
**Crew Chief:** The lead mechanic assigned to a plane. He is responsible for ensuring that the plane is mechanically sound and ready to fly on time.

**DO:** Director of operations. The second-in-command of the squadron. Watches the day-to-day flying activities of a squadron.

**Downrange:** Slang for flying into the combat zone, or AOR.

**DSN:** Military phone line for official calls. Free service. Can also use this phone to call home.

**ETOH:** Medical short-hand for alcohol. Booze, drink, the stuff that takes the pain away.

**E-1 to E-9**: The enlisted ranks.

**Front-end Crew:** The ones that fly the plane. The pilots, engineers, and loadmasters.

**Hard Broke:** Aircraft has a mechanical problem that is not easily fixed.

**Humvee:** The slang for the all-terrain vehicle now used by the US military. It replaced the Jeep in the 1980s. The Humvee is also known as the Hummer. The Humvee comes in a multitude of styles and configurations, and can carry four to ten people. The ambulance version can carry four litter patients.

**HRs:** Human remains. The politically correct modern military term for dead American soldiers.

**Garrison Life:** Stateside duty. Living within a regular fixed airbase. The opposite of living in the field or at a forward base.

**GI:** Slang from World War II to represent the common soldier, known as "government issue." It is not used often in the modern military. I use it in this book to refer to all the services that we care for: the army, navy, marines, air force, and coast guard.

**GSW:** Gunshot wound. Medical shorthand (e.g., "GSW to the head").

**Jump Orders:** A flight order that grants permission to travel on any military flight internationally. A free ticket to travel on official business.

**KIA:** Killed in Action. For military only, does not apply to the massive civilian army that is in Iraq.

**KP:** Kitchen Patrol. Enlisted additional duty of clean up detail at the chow hall. It is not desirable.

**Life Support:** a section that supplies and maintains all the emergency equipment for aircrews. This includes: helmets, chemical flying suits, survival vests, life jackets, escape and evasion equipment, and training.

**IV:** Intravenous fluids.

**NCO:** Non-commissioned officer. The rank of E-5 to E-9. The enlisted sergeant. The backbone of the military. The ones who get the actual work done.

**NOMEX/Flight suit:** Fire-resistant, one-piece suit that aircrew wear. The suit looks sharp, yet is hot in the heat of the desert.

**MASF:** Mobile aeromedical staging facility. Located close to a runway, the MASF holds up to fifty patients for four to six hours prior to aircraft departure. The MASF prepares patients for flight. The MASF in Kuwait was often overwhelmed with patients.

**MARS:** A network of civilian radios that support the military. By calling a Ham operator, a serviceman can establish a phone patch home.

**MCD:** Medical Crew Director. A flight nurse who is in charge of the medevac mission. Does not have to be the ranking officer on the crew. MCD is responsible for the safety and well being of the crew.

**MRE:** Meals ready to eat. The new modern field ration for the American military. Each meal is loaded with calories and can be eaten cold. MREs were issued in the first Gulf War and have improved in taste and variety for Iraqi Freedom. The MRE replaces the Vietnam-era C-ration. There are vegetarian and kosher versions.

**Mustang:** A military officer promoted from the ranks. Served enlisted prior to being commissioned. These officers often have a better understanding of working with the enlisted forces.

**PTSD:** Post-traumatic stress disorder. A condition that can occur after a traumatic life event. Sleepless nights, increased drinking, and anger are common symptoms of PTSD.

**RPG:** Rocket-propelled grenade. Different from a SAM because it is not guided.

**R&R:** Rest and Recuperation. Military slang for time off from war.

**SAM:** Surface-to-air missile. Either shoulder-fired, from a mobile platform, or from a fixed position. The missile can track an aircraft by radar or by sensing heat.

**Stage:** a forward location where aircraft and crews are positioned to operate. Planes and crews are staged to cut down on flying hours and reduce the duty day.

**Squadron:** The backbone organization of the air force. The functional unit. Each squadron has roughly 150-200 people assigned. The air force is structured in ascending order by flight, squadron, group, wing, numbered air force, and then by command.

**SP-** Security Police. The name has been changed to SF or Security Forces.

**TACC:** Tanker Airlift Control Center. The headquarters and command and control for the entire heavy airlift in the US Air Force. TACC is located in Scott AFB, Illinois. Because of time zone differences and because it is so far removed from the war zone, decisions often come late or are not in the best interest of the mission. Good communication and decision-making is a constant problem with TACC. Also called *MOTHER.*

**TDY:** Temporary duty assignment. Military jargon for being away from home station.

**Tube:** London's subway system.

**WIA:** Wounded in Action. Again, this only applies to the military and not the civilian contractors.

**Wing:** A large air force organization. Usually comprised of eight to ten squadrons and having three to four thousand people assigned.

**Zulu time, Z-time, or just Zulu:** The common time that all military aircraft work off of. We travel through so many time zones so quickly that everyone works on Z-time. Example: If I give a patient his six o'clock medication in Kuwait, what time does he need to take it in Germany?

# Bibliography

News bites – CNN.com and infoplease.com/spot/iraq-timeline

# Biography

**Ed Hrivnak, RN, BSN,** author of the journal *Medevac Missions,* is a professional fire officer for Central Pierce Fire and Rescue. *Medevac Missions* has appeared in the critically acclaimed anthology *Operation Homecoming* and the two-time Emmy winning film of the same name. The movie was nominated for several awards, including an Oscar for best documentary feature.

Part of his work is featured in the National Endowment of Humanities 2013 anthology *Standing Down.* This is a collection of significant works of military literature chosen to assist returning veterans with the transition to civilian life. The book comprises selections from literary giants that include Homer, Tolstoy, Lincoln, and Hemmingway.

Ed's words have been published in the *New Yorker,* the *Seattle Times,* the *Tacoma News Tribune,* the *Pittsburgh Post-Gazette,* and several international nursing journals. His war stories have aired on PBS, NPR, *ABC World News,* and numerous talk shows.

His writing was featured in theatrical presentations at Tacoma's Broadway Center for the Performing Arts, and the adaptation *Soldier's Circle* was performed at the University of Louisville.

Hrivnak was an instructor flight nurse in the Air Force Reserve. He retired as a captain after twenty years of service. A veteran of the first Gulf War and Operation Iraqi Freedom, Ed also participated in peacekeeping missions supporting Somalia, Rwanda, and the Balkans. Combining his military and civilian flying career, the author has logged over four thousand flight hours on twenty different types of aircraft. Much of his published work is based on treating casualties out of the Middle East.

Prior to retiring, Captain Hrivnak conducted research for the Assistant Surgeon General's Office of the US Air Force on the stress of caring for combat casualties. He has lectured at colleges, trauma conferences, and to international audiences on this subject.

The writer is married to nurse practitioner and three-tour veteran Lieutenant Colonel Jennifer Hrivnak. They live in the Pacific Northwest. The Hrivnaks have two young children, John Dawson and Shae Marie. Ed enjoys his time off with family, skiing, flying antique airplanes, and helicopters.